BACKGROUND PLAYER

Other published title by author:

Glamour and Turbulence (Vantage Press, 1996)

BACKGROUND PLAYER

Aimée Bratt

VANTAGE PRESS
New York

Jacket of "The Encounter" by Charity Blackstock used by permission of HarperCollins Publishers, Inc.

Cover design by Susan Thomas

FIRST EDITION

All rights reserved, including the right of
reproduction in whole or in part in any form.

Copyright © 2004 by Aimée Bratt

Published by Vantage Press, Inc.
419 Park Ave. South, New York, NY 10016

Manufactured in the United States of America
ISBN: 0-533-14547-3

Library of Congress Catalog Card No.: 2003090903

0 9 8 7 6 5 4 3 2 1

Contents

Preface	vii
1. New York 1970—A City in a Film Noir	1
2. Trials and Errors of the Portfolio Creation	7
3. Ansonia Hotel—"The Moments" (Acting Lessons)	11
4. Buddha	15
5. "The Second Coming"—Joining the Screen Actors Guild	21
6. "Testing" the Waters—Pictures and Résumés	25
7. Encounters of a Most Peculiar Kind	30
8. One Commercial after Another	35
9. Book Covers and Lingerie	40
10. Sylvia Fay—Casting Director of the Upscale	46
11. The Agony of Being an Extra	83
12. The Joy of the Upgrade	89
13. A Potpourri of Little Film Stories	93
14. Reading for a Part—Am I Wasting My Time?	101
15. Working with Woody	108
16. "Acting" like a "Stewardess"	113
17. Pains and Pleasures of the Period Movie	117
18. Films of the Nineties—A Different Look	122
19. Bernie from the Bronx and Other Characters	127
20. New York 2002–2003—a City Changed? The More It Stays the Same?	135

Preface

This book has been written for the three men I love, so that they would get a little more understanding of and some insight into my film work activities in New York during the last thirty years.

As for other readers, if there are any statements proven to be incorrect or inappropriate I apologize for the oversight. I have tried to be as truthful as possible. Any resemblance to any known person or persons, unless the real names have been used, is purely coincidental and not intended as such. Names have been changed in some cases for discretionary purposes.

This book is also not intended as some kind of general overview of a "trying to break into show business" tale. These are my personal stories, and they are purely autobiographical. Bear in mind that one need not be famous to write a book about show business. Everybody has something to say.

BACKGROUND PLAYER

1
New York 1970—A City in a Film Noir

I arrived in April. It was all very familiar to me. I had only been there twice before; nonetheless, it felt like coming home. The city had been awaiting me. It was oddly comforting, in contrast to the numerous accounts of overwhelming and intimidating experiences related by others, who lived there or had left. The rumors were so negative. In 1970 New York indeed had a very unfavorable reputation: crime-ridden, dirty, and unfriendly. "Why are you moving to New York? How could you live *there?*" But I knew better. I was attracted to its character, which I vaguely associated with a film noir. It was big and lonely, a fantasy in black and white, the streets and buildings hiding many secrets; there was drama and a gritty romance. If you could not understand that kind of imagination, perhaps then you would not enjoy living in New York. Especially at that time you needed a dose of rebellion to stand up against all the "smear campaign" about it. For example: "I hate the place!" "That city is a toilet!" (a comment in a film of the period). "I can't stand the people! I have never seen so much rudeness in my life!" These were mostly outsiders talking, but even inhabitants of New York would perpetually put it down in their clichéd "love-hate" relationship with the city.

I saw New York differently: the unique character, the history and the vintage facades, the Art Deco buildings, the powerful skyline, and the colorful New Yorkers with their wry and sardonic sense of humor. And what about the opportunities as far as careers and moneymaking that most definitely no other city in the whole world could offer? This was the city of many movies already made and would be in the upcoming years with directors like Martin Scorcese, Woody Allen, Coppola, and Sidney Lumet and actors such as Pacino, De Niro, and Joe Pesci and actresses such as Gena Rowlands and Meryl Streep and Glenn Close. These films were dramatic, realistic, and stark and gritty and maybe more worthy of one's attention than the generally "entertaining" Hollywood films of that time.

I had come from San Francisco in 1970 in order to change my domicile to New York as a Pan American flight hostess. I had had my fun of sun-filled layovers in the Pacific Islands, Hawaii, Tahiti, Guam, and the Far East, Hong Kong, Taipei, Tokyo, where I had spent some of the most exhilarating times of my life, flying for Pan American. I had loved the flying of the sixties, the alluring job that it was and would continue to be for a little while longer, a decade or two. However, that is another story, quite literally another book, which I wrote titled *Glamour and Turbulence—I Remember Pan Am—1966–1991*.

This account is not about flying or the airline business but about show business in New York but only in New York and my experiences in it at the lower tiers as a "background player" or bit player in New York–made features. The term *Background Player* has been used in the Screen Actors Guild's contract language, although the term "background actor" is the correct one. I also encountered other varieties of "playing in the background"—behind the scenes, no pun intended.

I had come to New York to expand on diverse activities, and what better place! Flying was no longer challenging enough, although I had no intention of quitting my job with all its privileges, time off, and still-enjoyable future trips to Europe, South America, and the Middle East as well as the Far East and Africa, where I had grown up. My father had been the Swedish envoy to Ethiopia in the fifties and later to Iran and Afghanistan in the sixties as well as to South Africa and much earlier in Berlin, Germany, as consul general some years after the war. I had grown up in these countries and as a consequence had learned to speak several foreign languages at an early age, skills that became instrumental when hired by Pan Am as well as useful to some extent in the pursuit of work in show business. My native country is Sweden, where I only lived ten years of my life, first at the ages of three to eight and the rest later in my teens, when I graduated from the French School in 1963, as well as from a commercial institute, called Schartau. I worked in a few jobs in marketing in Stockholm after that, and between attending the two schools I had also been a model in Paris on rue St. Honoré in a small fashion house, an eye-opening experience for me certainly.

The most significant part of growing up in different countries all over the world was the natural adaptation of the cultures of theses places and learning very quickly to be tolerant and view the world as it is viewed through the eyes of people who are different from you. We are not all alike, and I will never be able to understand why some individuals or groups of people in this world cannot leave others alone. We are different, products of our environments, our genes. Nationality, race, religion—I see intolerance in all categories. When I grew up, it was second nature to me, the dissimilarities. So?! Don't impose your standards or beliefs on others. Or worse, your morals or your religion!

Back to New York. This was the city where, in my view, tolerance of diverse cultures was most practiced.

I threw myself into an array of activities: dancing lessons (I had taken ballet and jazz before), cooking lessons at the YWCA (very inexpensive at the time), and philosophy lessons at Hunter College. This philosophy class was too large, I thought, the teacher capable but ineffectual, and the students very undisciplined, compared, anyway, to the strict schooling I had been accustomed to. We all wrote a paper about Plato and almost everyone got a B! Why only Plato? What about all the other philosophers in history?

I also "checked out" as in-flight purser for Pan Am, a job on the plane with increased responsibilities. The 747s had now come into service. Flying with the ensuing deregulation took on another look. Gone were the elegance, the romance, the heyday of flying. Enter a new breed of passengers and service for them. The standards were lowered. At Pan Am, though, we still flew all over the world, and in spite of all the trials with this airline, we continued to have the best of times.

I settled down in New York with very little difficulty. My first humble apartment was on Third Avenue and 65th Street, a dingy little walk-up with furniture from the Salvation Army and infested with my new co-tenants—roaches everywhere! There was inadequate heat, and I froze through the first winter. I had to turn the oven on for warmth, a dangerous practice, a fire hazard. I did not think much about that, for now I had met someone. I was completely surprised and unprepared for this, because I had not come to New York to meet yet another man, for I had just broken off an affair. My mind wanted clear-sightedness, not another emotional upheaval. I wanted to do things with my head, not my heart.

Soon, I settled down into a beautiful new apartment in the east thirties—sedate Murray Hill, where I have lived ever since. Now I loved New York!

The next step would be show business? I was not interested in acting at all, certainly not stage work. How could I pursue a career like that? I was flying and could never give up that kind of security. I knew full well that acting was serious business and required a full commitment to acting lessons, voice lessons, and the pursuit of the "business" angle, i.e., contacting agents, casting directors, and photographers, printing résumés, et cetera. I could not be away half of the month on trips. Furthermore, I had a Swedish or at least a European accent, which at times would prove to be an asset, however, most of the time was very limiting.

I was twenty-seven years old, at the time too old for ingenue roles. It was actually the modeling jobs I was after. I had done it before in Paris as well as some showroom modeling in San Francisco. Nonetheless, it was a rather foolish desire on my part. Although I had quite a good figure, my face was not model material. Perhaps I could get away with a little commercial printwork?

I did not quite know how to proceed and had to rely on either good or bad advice, the consequence of which I will tell you about in the coming chapters. I got a tremendous amount of bad advice, which during the ensuing years I learned to ignore and even ridicule. What people do and say to get your attention!

However, one good piece of advice I got was to take

acting lessons—in addition to all my other lessons! I was now a very busy lady! In 1970 you were either a Successful Model, an Aspiring Model, or an Actress Struggling To Make It or you could settle for something in between, a vague middle position of Model/Actress-To-Be. There was nothing wrong with that, provided you had an income on the side, lots of time on your hands, and took the business in stride and rolled with the punches. I had all three or at least the first two! As far as rolling with the punches, my following stories are examples of the good, the bad, and sometimes the ugly.

So I tried out for the model/actress venture, and what a journey it became! I could not have imagined at the time that these moonlight activities would last into the twenty-first century. I never regretted them.

2
Trials and Errors of the Portfolio Creation

As I settled down in the city, I almost immediately started this undertaking on the path to a modeling career, and the first step was to ask questions. Some people told me to forget about it—it was too competitive. Others said I should give it a try, and that meant doing "the rounds" of the modeling agencies, both big and small. However, in order to do that I had to acquire pictures of myself, and quite a variety of them. So enter the photographers. The city had a million and one photographers, some very good, and then there were the very mediocre, and there were a few rather despicable characters I came across.

The first one I was introduced to had at one time been a celebrity photographer by the name of Peter Basch, who had photographed stars such as Marlene Dietrich and others many years ago. He had his studio in the middle of the city on the West Side somewhere. I had been referred to him by the husband of a Norwegian Pan Am colleague, who had an influential position at NBC. His name was André de Szekely, and he became a very good friend, one of the people I have memories of during those first few years of my introduction to New York in the early seventies. He sent me to Peter Basch. "Go to him! He takes fantastic pictures!" André said in his Hungarian accent.

Before I had met Peter Basch, I had managed to scrape together some pictures of modeling poses taken by some unremembered individual. Since I had done runway jobs in San Francisco and been a "house model" in Paris, I had only a vague idea of what so-called test shots were supposed to look like. When I trotted up to Basch's studio with these pictures in hand, he took one look at them and exclaimed, "These are *ludicrous!*" This word I had never heard before. The term *ludicrous* thus became part of my vocabulary from then on. It was used a lot in New York in the seventies; I don't know why!

So, I proceeded to pose for Basch in bathing suits and various outfits of the period. There were both midi- and maxi-skirts, a lot of leather fringes, sunglasses (big round ones), long hairpieces, and those annoying fake eyelashes that were always coming off and had to be reglued and reglued.

As a favor to André, Peter Basch did these pictures for me, I think, and that was very courteous of him. Some of the shots were used in newspaper columns in the *New York Post* by Earl Wilson and Martin Burden, where I was mentioned: "Swedish Actress Aimée Bratt said at Nichols she'll be in the Felix Mendelsson film `Wedding March' " and "Aimée Bratt said at Ponte's she'll be in Albert Finney's film `Wolfen,' " as well as "Swedish born Aimée Bratt" and "airline stewardess" A.B. said she will be "playing an airline stewardess" in a variety of films in all kinds of restaurants, accompanied by all these Basch bathing suit photos on at least five different occasions! It was only publicity for the films and the restaurants. As for me, the only benefit was a few copied displays in my new "model portfolio," which would serve somewhat to my advantage.

The portfolio was to take shape far off in the future, however, after many, many photographer test shots. These photo sessions were made for the benefit of both the photographer and the model. The photographer could possibly use them, and the model needed as many as possible in order to get started in the business. The test shots were large prints made from proofs, hundreds and hundreds of them, in these sessions and then placed in the model portfolio for presentation to the many ad agencies and at the so called go-sees, when you went to see all kinds of casting people, hoping for possible bookings. This was awfully time consuming. I later found out that you were sent out randomly by an agency, whether or not you were right for the job. It did not matter to them, because you were never paid a dime for it! You would be sent along sometimes with hundreds of other models for the same go-see, all made up as for a booking and dressed accordingly, with portfolio in tow, to be displayed and spend only maybe two minutes with the person, who only hired one model, and then be dismissed with a "we'll call you" rejection. It was the way the business worked; the model's time had no value, and of course you were rarely taken seriously. At least I had another occupation, and a good one at that.

Now, with the few pictures that I had put together with the help of Basch, he sent me to the Wilhelmina modeling agency, at that time one of the top ones along with Ford. He had gotten this idea that I resembled my compatriot a Swedish model famous for the soap commercial with the line "take it all off." She was managed by "Willie."

Wilhelmina had been an extremely successful model

in the sixties, with a slew of *Vogue* covers, and now she headed her own very elite agency. I was led into her office. She was very beautiful, spoke with a slight German accent, and smoked quite a few cigarettes. She looked at my pictures very quickly and expertly and just stated matter-of-factly; "Yes, he was right [Peter Basch]. You do look like her, but I can't do anything for you. I would send you both for the same job, and she would not like that, I know." She shook her head a little and then added in a somewhat distracted tone of voice, "You can go and see this person [she mentioned a name]. . . . Maybe he can do something for you."

I wrote down the information, thanked her, and said good-bye. Before I proceeded further with that particular advice, I did the rounds of just a few more agencies, but without much zest or luck, because I now realized and was warned that many of these were scams. They wanted money up front for the privilege of being pictured in their agency book, for which there was no guarantee, or they would send you to photographers who were far from professional and make you pay for useless pictures. So in the beginning I got no portfolio or worthwhile experience to speak of.

I heeded Wilhelmina's advice to go and see that particular person. Let's call him Mr. Black. I think he had very dark eyes, black? It turned out to be one of the most bizarre encounters in the city, yet quite typical of New York in the seventies, if you will. But there would be a silver lining!

3
Ansonia Hotel—"The Moments" (Acting Lessons)

I don't remember if it was Mr. Black or someone else in 1970 or '71 who advised me to take acting lessons. I will, however, return later to Mr. Black and the silver lining, namely, Buddha, code name for a person, who became entirely instrumental and important in my life. Ansonia Hotel was really something out of a film noir, in my imagination at least. It is a beautiful old building on the Upper West Side on Broadway and 72d Street, famous for its various artistic activities of dance, music, and song. You could hear opera sung there. Also, it served as a kind of home for residents in the area, who if not exactly homeless, had a certain Runyonesque flavor about them. In the early seventies you could see them in the lobby: alcoholics, bums, social cast-asides. The women could be quite colorful, garish-looking aging prostitutes with brassy bleached hair and too-tight skirts over flabby bellies and thighs.

We, that is, a little "cast" of would-be actors, all young people from a variety of diverse backgrounds, would meet there, in the lobby, and proceed into the room next to it. There was a real stage to perform on and many chairs. It was used for showcases and our acting classes. This was called the Actors Mobile Theatre and headed by our acting coach, Brett Warren. To me, this was truly a real New York experience, maybe the most significant one I will ever have, and it very often floats back into my conscience. In that Ansonia Hotel there was such an atmosphere of drama and mystery, very hard to describe to people who would never be part of it.

The next ten months I would be "performing" here and, I think, no doubt would come as close to acting as I ever will. Brett Warren had allegedly been blacklisted during the McCarthy era and had never really gotten over it, as I understood it. At that time he suffered somewhat from a medical condition and could become quite agitated when we did not concentrate on our work. It was the Stanislavsky Method, of course, that we were studying. I had not heard of the Method before, but I was quickly introduced into this technique and into exercising my skills at the Moment, an acting performance in which you remember a "moment" of importance to you. This moment could be very minor, but you had to relive it and perform it onstage, making the scene thought-provoking and significant.

Brett Warren was wonderful, although I experienced him as more of an intriguing, even enigmatic personality than an acting coach. I "acted" out many "moments" in those classes, most out of my own intuition rather than on his guidance. How do you demonstrate a moment? You show your audience the situation you were in, including significant details (could be a wind blowing), and convey the emotions felt at the time. You replay the scene: showing sadness and weeping, trembling with fear, dancing for joy, protesting in anger—you are a comedian; you become sexy! I once acted "on the airplane," describing moments of confrontations with unruly passengers, a "show" that was met with surprisingly amused acceptance.

My co-actors became my close friends, and I will never forget them. They were real New Yorkers, and my memories of especially Karen and Aldo (not his real name) are still with me after thirty years. Karen was working on Wall Street. She was Italian-American, short, lively, brunette, and very talented, a real comedienne. Aldo was also Italian-American. I did many scenes with him, and we were probably a good couple in acting class. I was a little attracted to him, not only because he was good-looking and talented but also because he had an aura of secrecy about him, an elusiveness, a moodiness, troubled. I later found out he was very troubled indeed. I had invited him to join me and some friends for dinner. He wanted very much to stay with us, but after just a little while at the restaurant table he had to excuse himself. He was very, very sick. It was heroin all along. Karen had tried to tell me about it. He seemed to get worse and worse, and he could no longer perform in acting class. I don't know what became of him, but I just remember him as a very romantic and tragic acting partner.

Brett Warren was also getting worse, his illness leaving him quite ineffectual in the end. Once I got perturbed with him because after my scenes he would say nothing, no critique, not a word. What was I doing wrong? I was surprised to hear from him, at a later time that he valued "my work" a whole lot and I should not be concerned, just continue with my "craft." Sadly, shortly thereafter he had to stop, and my acting lessons would cease. Anyway, I have one most amusing story about him:

One time we, Karen and I, were invited along with Brett Warren to attend a play somewhere in the city. We were seated in a row right behind a lady with a rather large and wide-brimmed hat. Brett was a little annoyed, because his view was partially obstructed. Karen and I thought it humorous and soon had to suppress our titters. The more the play proceeded, the angrier Brett would get. The play was very important to him, and at one moment, a critical one, he could not see properly because of this hat, so he started to gesticulate with his hands, shaking with irritation, and exclaimed rather loudly, "Lady, would you please remove your *head!*"

We finally did a showcase at Ansonia, and many people came to see us perform. I did a scene with Aldo, and the audience clapped.

This was, however, not the first time I had been onstage. During my growing-up years I did school plays, just like everyone else. What was a little different about them was the fact that they were done in all kinds of international schools all over the world. For instance, I played the leading singing part in *The Princess and the Swinekeeper* in Berlin in 1953. I sang, "Ach du lieber Augustin, Augustin . . . alles ist weg," and was praised with flowers and curtain calls at the age of ten! When I grew up in Africa, we did Shakespeare plays, which were part of the curriculum in this very British school. I played the lead in one and had to memorize pages and pages of lines. It was quite a feat. However, the rather stern schoolmaster, after listening to me at a rehearsal, yelled out from somewhere in the dimly lit room, *"I can't hear a word you're saying! Is it some kind of foreign language?"*

4
Buddha

Heeding Wilhelmina's advice, I went to see Mr. Black. He was tall and dark, and his apartment-cum-office was filled with a messy array of wires and equipment of all sorts, extending all over the floors from wall to wall and in the corners. I climbed over some of it and plunked myself down on a sofa. He started to "interview" me in a rather laconic way. He was somber and a little cynical, saying, about New York, "What do you want from this town? I like London. Here every street and every block looks the same!" Well, I sure did not think so. He acted as if he did not quite know what to do with me and gave me an address to yet another small modeling agency. Meanwhile, he proceeded to show me pictures of various successful models, saying, "This was my girlfriend," or, "I am dating this one." The photos were spectacular, and it was obvious that he wanted to impress and boast about it all and give me tall tales.

Then he did something very odd. He laid down on the sofa and asked me to massage his hipbone! I flatly refused; "What on earth for?" I took it in stride, though, and gave him another chance.

After visiting that agency he sent me to with a questionable outcome, I went back to see Mr. Black, who now informed me that the person heading the agency had been lukewarm about my chances for success in the modeling field and I would probably not make any "big money" for him.

So what were we going to do now? "The next five years will be the same as your last five years!" he said again in that offhand monotone. What on earth did he know about my last five years?! I got annoyed. However, this was a little typical of the early seventies. Individuals who thought of themselves as being in powerful positions often made judgments and patronizing evaluations about young women. This was early in the feminist era, and you would just sort of sit there and listen to their oratory about themselves and plenty of mediocre advice as how to proceed into show business. Mr. Black, however, was not all offensive, like others I would meet later. He was just a little negative in his outlook, and as far as his hipbone mattered, he could be excused.

Then all of a sudden he exclaimed, "I think I will send you to G.C.! *But he is crazy!*" Ah, there was the silver living. The minute he said that, my curiosity immediately took flight, followed by a generally positive feeling of what was to come. Here was the end of the tunnel, a ray of light. It was purely my intuition.

The address was on 57th Street between Lexington and Third Avenue in the middle of the block, a postwar building. Here I went up to the eighteenth floor, all the way into the corner, number 18G. I knocked on the door; a voice said "Enter!" I opened the door, and there was Buddha, with a large cigar, sitting behind a large desk, cluttered with albums, papers and pens, and a telephone. The room was very small, but with plenty of people in it. Models and actresses of all types and shapes were sitting on two leather couches and a few chairs flanked by a number of male characters, men in the business or of various associations. The room was full of smoke from cigarettes and Buddha's cigar. There was a balcony right behind Buddha, and the door to it was ajar. Buddha cracked a big smile on a face that was round and very jolly, with big eyes that seemed to be forever amused at the world and twinkled with mischief, however benign. You just saw the top of his body above the desk, wonderfully obese. Buddha was an institution, and he was now holding court.

He looked at me and spoke very quickly and wittily: "Oh yes, I'll send you to some people. You are a Jeanne Moreau type! Can't promise anything, though. You are a little too sophisticated, see, very European, too formal."

Almost immediately he gave me a piece of paper with names and addresses of photographers, casting directors, and people in ad agencies, along with all the phone numbers, very detailed and organized. "Call them up, all of them! You have to get a portfolio, see, like they all have in here," and he pointed to the other girls, some of them very stunning to look at, sitting there with their "books" (portfolios) in various shades of black and brown. "Call up this photographer; he is the *best!* He'll take good pictures, very good. And call me tomorrow!"

I sat down for a while to listen to this demonstration of a one-man show. He was Buddha, he was holding court, and this was his entourage, his protegées, the models, certainly not all high-fashion. They were "actresses" also being courted by these New York characters, some of whom were legitimate photographers, others who called themselves producers in the business, whether they were or not, and then close friends of Buddha or just hangers-on. The conversation, or shall we say Buddha's monologue, consisted mostly of raucous sex talk, outrageous, funny, outspoken, wild, and crazy, as Mr. Black had said. Now, Buddha was a curious individual. He asked questions between his own statements like, "Which position do you prefer?" and, "Why are men so fond of oral sex, and what about women?" He would carry the discussion to the scientific levels of the Master and Johnson teachings about orgasms, and so on and on.

The models/actresses, however, were there to get work in show business from him, and he did have a tremendous amount of contacts with producers and directors and casting people. They had concerns of another nature: what could he do for them? Invariably, more often than not, when they proceeded with, "Can I ask you a question?" he unblinkingly replied cheerfully, "Six inches!"

Well now, Buddha, with that kind of humor, did not appeal to everyone, but if you went along with this low-life jargon, which was harmless, and allowed yourself to be amused, you ended up having a "jolly" good time. I did sooner rather than later begin to benefit greatly from this new-won friendship. Because that was what Buddha became, a great new confidant and ally to me, supporter, and comforter. You see, Buddha had a great big heart!

For the next twenty years or so I would be in daily contact with him, and he became responsible for my entering into the Screen Actors Guild, working in New York–made films and TV and commercials and so-called industrials, hundreds and hundreds of times during those years, as well as quite a few model or printwork bookings in the beginning of the seventies, another angle of the business, and ultimately, perhaps best of all, would be receiving a Screen Actors Guild pension later on as well as medical insurance.

I was lucky with Buddha. He never made a "pass" at me. He did, however, have a dubious reputation. Young girls, out-of-towners, would come to him, and of course they were naive. What did they know? In spite of his good heart, and he *did* help them, if he was able, he, nonetheless, propositioned them in a frank manner: "If you want me to help you, you have to do this for me. . . ." The girls obliged more often than not. This was thirty years ago! The majority of them ended up being disappointed, of course. If you could not make a living in New York, you could not stay, and the jobs were scarce. Buddha sent them to people in the industry, but it was mostly up to themselves to become successful; and some did quite well.

As for me, I had no problems with Buddha. I had my job with Pan Am, so I was never "needy" for show business or making money. I also had my steady friend who met with Buddha also at those in-house sessions on 57th Street. One time Buddha made the remark about me: "She does not turn me on!" and we laughed and laughed. It was my European accent, he said. Sure!

As the years went by, as I have said, he was my friend and would comfort me and cheer me up during telephone conversations when I was upset or sad. He was a master at turning the negative into the positive like no one else I have ever known. He was always there for me. He was inspirational and always happy and made you feel good about yourself. "You have nothing to worry about!" he said, and that was his philosophy. It worked very well at the time. He also said to me something that still works today. "Three good things about you: You don't have a petty bone in your body, you are a woman of your word, and you are one of the world's greatest lovers!" Only he and I knew what he meant.

The following are accounts and little stories of the jobs in the film business, TV, and elsewhere, all with the encouragement of Buddha.

5
"The Second Coming"—Joining the Screen Actors Guild

Shortly after I met Buddha, he sent me to go and see someone down in the Village. His name was Bob Madero, a gentle and rather young film producer and director who was working on his first film. It was to be called *The Second Coming* (of Christ). It was a so-called low-budget venture and very typical of the early seventies. This was in August 1971, and I remember the first meeting with him. It was in his apartment; he was talking about his work and then gave me the script to look at, just briefly. He needed some players for a party scene that would turn violent. He thought I would fit in very well as a Swedish model type, clad in "hot pants," the fashion of that period, along with long blond hair and platform shoes. I would also speak a few lines in a Swedish accent. He was going to give me a "principal player" contract. This piece of paper was the most important document for me in order to acquire the coveted membership in the Screen Actors Guild. You *had* to be in the guild to get any legitimate work in the show business. Everything else was not quite "legit," was less of a credit on a résumé, and did not pay very much at all, if anything. The Screen Actors Guild guaranteed that you were paid on time and according to scale and got fair treatment on the set. It was the actors' union.

Bob Madero did not tell me very much about the film except to show up for this particular scene, dressed for it as we had discussed, and just "be myself." There was nothing in the script for me, so he was going to give me a few lines impromptu, as the filming proceeded, to fit my character.

This was to be my first film experience, and I had no idea what to expect. As soon as I arrived in the early morning for the "shoot," I was introduced to the other actors, the major players and the minor ones, who greeted me with a slight gesture of indifference. Then the long wait began. We sat there and waited and waited and waited all day long! Much too early in the game I inquired as to what we were doing there. "This is the way *it is* in movies!" someone said impatiently. What kind of a question was that? From a novice! From that moment on I understood very well that making a film is a lengthy drawn-out procedure, because of all the technical labor of setting up the lights and the camera and all the endless adjustments of creating a scene, wrapping it all up, and starting building another one.

Sometime in the afternoon we were finally placed on the set. I had on my hot pants, some kind of blue shimmering blouse, platform sandals, and the hair hanging straight down. I was twenty-seven years old and I would play this model in this party scene, in which we were all to be killed, something à la the Manson murders a few years earlier, that horror still fresh. When I later watched this low-budget feature on the big screen, Bob Madero's big project, I found it to be quite an intriguing film. I just thought the editing could have been a little less erratic. There was a lot of sex and nudity in the film, again typical of the seventies. I had been concerned about that little problem at first and had told Buddha that I would not do nude scenes in any film or on other jobs, for that matter. What would Pan Am say!?

Nudity was the cause of much discussion among models and actresses and casting people. It was a controversial topic, whether to do nude scenes, or partial nudes, how much exposure or how little, and under what circumstances. Nudity was acceptable to some as long as it was perceived as being in "good taste." Well, I eventually learned to distinguish between the good taste and the bad taste of the casting people themselves who were involved.

However, when Bob Madero interviewed me he had been very up-front and truthful, informing me that only the starring players would do nudity, which turned out to be the case indeed.

Now the scene in *The Second Coming* was up. I was placed on a sofa and would be chatting with a male actor, some kind of ad-libbed conversation. There were several shots taken of us from all angles. We were all party people, drinking and having a good time. After a while the party turned more frenzied. I think there was simulated pot smoking, and what else? All of a sudden I felt a stab in my back. I had been knifed. We all tumbled on top of one another, falling all over one another and getting quite bruised as a result. There were screams, more knife attacks, and more screams. I think we did only one take of this scene. It was acceptably realistic, which was very much due to the fact that we had been overcome with surprise. We knew the knife attacks would occur, but not quite at which point. The knives were toy knives, and there was "blood" all over the place. It was quite rough, and I was left with those bruises for a while, an acute reminder of my introduction to film work. I did not mind.

I still have the letter/contract from Dobbs Ferry Films, the production company. I had been a "principal on camera," and now I was eligible to join the Screen Actors Guild. At that time you also had to pay an entry fee of about six hundred dollars, which was a very big sum indeed. I managed to scrape that together. Now I had my foot in the door.

6
"Testing" the Waters—Pictures and Résumés

My next job for Buddha would be a disastrous part on the popular TV show *To Tell the Truth*. I was to "play" an imposter of June Collins, the author of a book about corruption and bribery committed by certain Vietnam army officers. She had been called upon to testify against them.

Now, I knew nothing about the American military, and here I was supposed to answer questions about the Vietnam War on this game show. I was completely miscast. Naturally, I got very few votes and was at the end identified as a Pan Am flight stewardess. Ironically, I had flown in and out of Vietnam many times on the so-called (Rest and Recuperation) flights, transporting soldiers back and forth. These flights were operated by Pan Am for several years. It was typical of Buddha to send you into some kind of job just in order to give you camera exposure and experience on a stage. When you later complained that it had been embarrassing, he would laugh and chuckle with amusement.

On to better and bigger things. I had joined the

Screen Actors Guild, namely SAG, and now the time had come to produce a résumé and a working "head shot." That was what you needed to present to all the casting people, ad agencies, casting directors, and commercial agents.

As far as the résumé went, all I could place on it was my credit from *The Second Coming* and my acting lessons with Actors Mobile Theatre (Brett Warren). *To Tell the Truth* would have to be included as well, and a few modeling experiences did not hurt. Some concocted make-believe acting roles à la Buddha were added on just for looks.

I spent the next few years, still the early seventies, doing so-called test shoots with numerous photographers. You had to constantly update your model portfolio, the book for presentation to casting people and printwork agencies, as well as the more important head shot for acting jobs, which was attached to the résumé. This picture/résumé became your calling card. You had to send out hundreds and hundreds of these eight-by-ten photos in the mail to all the casting people. A lot of postage! Later on it also became common practice to send out smaller versions of the pictures, postcard-size, usually without a résumé (too small), as reminders that you were still in the business and available for work. It was almost a full-time job to keep up with this undertaking of going after the jobs, the auditions, the calling on photographers, go-sees for potential bookings, interviews with casting directors and reading for them (if you were lucky enough to be asked!), and those awful cattle calls. I had to do it all part-time between my flights, and I was flying to Tokyo a few times a month! In the beginning I was also busy with my acting classes and ballet and jazz classes. Something had to give.

After flying in from Tokyo on a fourteen-hour nonstop flight I would go straight to acting class. I was falling asleep all over the place. I finally gave up all the classes.

Now Buddha started sending me to photographers, one after the other, for all of these test shots. I did so many sessions that I have several books filled with these pictures along with hundreds and hundreds of copies, some of which I threw out as the years went by. Everybody who was a model or actress or actor had a million pictures! It got to be very tiresome, especially talking about them, what was wrong with your face, your hair, your expression. The picture was not "commercial" enough, too much smiling there, too dark, too light, too dramatic, too young, too old . . .

"This head shot does not look like you!" "How long ago was this taken? You need to update it." "You can do without all that smiling!" "I think you should do your hair more blonde." "You look like a doll here, too plastic!" "There is no expression in the eyes." The head shot was supposed to look a little bit better than you did in order to sell you faster. That strategy did not always work, though. "Your picture looks better than *you!*"

One of my first photo sessions was with Sam Harte, a really nice man, who took glamorous pictures in color. It was evening gowns and bathing suits and hot pants and costume jewelry. You did your own makeup as well as the hair, which was changed, up or down, as the shooting went on. He took several rolls of film and asked you to pose in different attitudes. He was easy to work with, very kind, and you quickly learned what effect was desirable.

The photographers were all different. Some wanted hip pictures, others more sexy, sometimes nudity or only the insinuation thereof. It had to benefit them as well as the model. That was the deal, since nobody got paid for the work.

The good photographers I worked with were Al Karp, Sam Costello, Bill Stone, George Lockhart, Warren Flagler, Bob Lichtman, and many others. However, Valentin was the photographer I enjoyed working with most of all. He was a warmhearted Brazilian who took especially glamorous shots and made you look good. I had a special rapport with him, but then again, he loved women. This was not true about some of the others.

Other photographers were testy, quite rude, temperamental, impatient, and difficult to work with, and not surprisingly, the pictures did not turn out well. They could be mediocre, the strain on your face would show, or the image would not reflect the model. These sessions could also be nothing more than "experiments" at best, valuable only to the photographer. "Comb your hair!" one would say, after I had already done it. One model was asked to sit on the floor in her seven-hundred-dollar suit. This was a job, so she said, "Why should I sit on the floor in my seven-hundred-dollar suit for a one-hundred-dollar job!"

"This is your competition!" another one growled at a friend of mine, pointing to a catalog of model pictures. She did not need to be reminded of the obvious.

Then there were the endless discussions about nude versus nonnude. Many photographers wanted to do nude shots, for it was beneficial for them. In order to sell or use the pictures, the signature and the permission of the model were required, but more often than not the photographers got away with selling the photos in foreign countries or to underground operators. At that time I never heard of any legal actions or suits. Consequently, they would often pressure you to take your clothes off, and sometimes you stripped a little just for the sake of peace. We were in our twenties, and at that time, right after the sixties, nudity seemed to be far less of a production, not such a big deal, compared to today, when, in my view, attitudes have grown outright prudish.

One such time was "on location" outside in upstate New York. I found myself sitting in knee-high grass, and there were mosquitoes. This photographer was asking me repeatedly to pull down the top of my summer dress. I did not feel like doing that at all. He finally became so frustrated that he approached me and suddenly kind of yanked the dress down in one simple sweep. Now I was more or less obscured by the high grass, so I let it go at that. The shots came out quite beautiful, because it looked like something out of an Ingmar Bergman film, and I ended up appreciating them. However, next time nudity would happen with my permission.

The next time was a very unusual and interesting session. There were three photographers. I was to be painted all white, like the girl in *Goldfinger,* and the idea intrigued me. I did not mind doing nude shots in such a situation. I would be covered with paint anyway! And it was fun! We did all these creations with white limbs and my chalky face (like a geisha) and poses like statues. The four of us were experimenting with all these contortions and dance postures and movements, some only of me and some with one or two of them. This was certainly in "good taste," no pressure here whatsoever, and very enjoyable to boot.

7
Encounters of a Most Peculiar Kind

Buddha was crazy!

Buddha had a little game he liked to play at the expense of almost everyone. He enjoyed arranging meetings between people for the sake of pure amusement, regardless of the outcome. Like a mischievous kid he would tell some casting director that he was sending over a "most talented" actress to read for a part when in fact she was a totally inexperienced young girl from out of town. Sometimes this led to disastrous consequences in the form of embarrassment; but more often than not the girl would receive a little exposure and learn how to proceed in the future. Buddha could be so outrageous. Once, for instance, he sent someone who had a cold to see a plastic surgeon! He was a doctor, wasn't he? They knew each other, of course, and in those days people seemed to have more time to waste. Buddha just got away with these charades, and those who knew him just shook their heads and laughed it off.

In the seventies, however, New York was inhabited by, shall we say, many sexually perverse individuals, and you had to watch your step. Like someone remarked,

"There are a lot of horny people in this town!" Well, they all had a story, too. They were human!

So here I was, unsuspecting at first, jumping into taxis (it was very cheap then), off to one "interview" after another, sometimes two or three a day. I met all kinds of characters, some friends of Buddha in the business and others legitimate casting directors and film producers. Now Buddha had a reputation. He was a manager, a personal one, who introduced you to casting people for the purpose of getting work in show business for us, the aspiring actresses. He was also known, by some, as a go-between for the purpose of "arrangements" of a different kind, subject to your imagination. But as I have said, he was a jokester, and what is wrong with giving people a good time? He never did a spiteful thing, he just did "introductions." You could take it from there!

New York at that time was a very exciting place to dwell, and you had plenty of choices. It was up to you. So what if you ended up looking a little foolish at times?

I have not exactly regretted any moments of Buddha's go-sees with the people "of a peculiar kind" whom I encountered, because they were all part of the story. The prim and prissy need not apply. Here are a few samples of what I have remembered:

One of the first people Buddha sent me to see was a gentleman who was very influential in show business, an associate of a casting director. He did not do any casting himself but would pretend as if he did. He had no job offers at all but claimed to be an authority on how to audition for a part. When you went to see him, you sat in a selected chair and listened (before you knew better!) for up to an hour to his oratory about himself, his opinions, and what one had to do to get "ahead" in show business. It all amounted to, of course, nothing more than a demand for a sexual favor by this gentleman. After several years he became a laughingstock, but I am sure he "scored" many a time. Buddha later told me that it was demeaning to be propositioned like that but also to have to spend the time listening to such a person. It was the worst kind of ego massaging, a terrible waste of time. It could not even qualify as the "casting couch" syndrome, because there was no casting involved!

This person was not the only one. I learned soon enough to stay at these meetings for a shorter time and quickly excused myself if nothing materialized as far as work. Nonetheless, you were polite. Today courtesy is not regarded as being quite so necessary.

Another person I was to be interviewed by was a rather distinguished businessman staying at one of the more elegant hotels in town. This rendezvous was like a flat joke. He was soon trying to have a date with me. I was trying to get a job. "You take care of me," he said, "and I'll take care of Buddha." I must have spent a half hour there, arguing. He sent me home in a taxi and gave me twenty dollars, a good amount in those days!

One of the most shocking encounters I experienced happened in the middle of the day, behind closed doors, and, believe it or not, in one of the top advertising agencies on Madison Avenue. I had gone there to read for a TV commercial. It was a young guy who suddenly out of the blue made a pass at me and tried physically to overpower me, and in such an awkward way. Talk about a "hostile takeover!" Can you imagine the lawsuit over sexual harassment today? I got out of there fast. Even Buddha was surprised.

Once Buddha committed another "hit and misdeed." He called up this supposed film director and told him there were "two very talented Swedish actresses" he was sending over, me, and a friend of mine who was just visiting town. She trotted along agreeably. When we arrived, there was indeed a script, but it turned out to be pure porn! Buddha actually did this now and then, and inevitably some women got the parts in these kind of films.

At that time, the Mafia allegedly produced and financed many New York–made features, and one of them was rumored to be *The Valachi Papers*. Buddha knew some of the casting people involved with the film, and I was sent to see one person in particular, who was indeed a very important casting director in New York. I was going to be interviewed for the part of a dead call girl, whether that suited me or not!

It was an old building somewhere on the West Side. I walked up some stairs and was ushered into a large room, very seedy-looking, where some people were sitting on chairs randomly, waiting. I sat down also. Everybody was strangely quiet, some whispering. They were all men; I don't remember any women. This was a peculiar casting call.

After quite a while someone called me into this even larger room. There were velvet curtains suspended all over the walls and the windows, burgundy red with gold tassels, and ornate chairs and sofas. Very Baroque. What was this? Marquis de Sade? Somewhat ominous-looking characters were leaning against the walls, looking bored but watchful. The old man by the desk was quite friendly and spoke in a raspy voice. I was in there for maybe ten minutes. This casting director was, shall we say, awesome in his capacity. He showed respect for you up until a certain moment. First he spoke of the film, the scene with the call girl and so on, but then he did a rather odd thing. He pointed to his crotch and explained that he had just had an operation and complained that "it" was just out of commission!

I offered my sympathies and left shortly thereafter.

A wonderful man I met in the business, and of course also through Buddha, was a very well-known casting director in New York by the name of Louis DiGiaimo. He cast *The Godfather,* I believe all of the parts except the stars. I went to see him several times and did get work off and on. He had a beard and was very soft-spoken and looked at you peering with lively, intelligent, and amused eyes. A friend of mine said, "Stroke his beard; he likes that!" Buddha adored him, and the feeling was, I am sure, mutual. He is still a major casting director in New York and casts only principal roles.

One individual whom I met turned out to be, if not so peculiar, a pleasure: Joe Franklin, the late-night TV host. Buddha sent me to see him, because he would use people on his show for fun and entertainment, especially for humorous interviews.

His office was a sight to behold: Books and papers mounted on top of his desk and stacked all the way up by the walls into the ceiling. There were a million pictures, and now he got mine, too. He just talked and talked very quickly. What a New Yorker! I don't quite remember what he asked me to do for his show. It was something to do with being a flight hostess for Pan Am. I would have declined that. Publicity was not allowed without Pan Am's permission, and getting that would have been too much of a complicated undertaking. It didn't quite fit. I was now leading a double life, and flying and filming did not mix!

8
One Commercial after Another

My next job with Buddha would be a very small part in another low-budget venture, produced by a friend of his called Martin Stayden and titled *I Could Never Go to Bed with a Man Who Has No Respect for My Husband*. It was to be shot on Martha's Vineyard. I was introduced to Mr. Stayden, and although he could not promise me a speaking part, there would be a close-up of my face.

The day came, and I went out there accompanied by another girl, who was also cast in a small role. She would be a stuntwoman. She and I shared a room at a local motel, and we ended up having quite a good time in this beautiful area. The weather was cold and damp, though. Martin Stayden was true to his word; my close-up was done. When I later watched it on the screen, it was not too bad, however, not too good, either. I looked a little "windblown!" The film was typical of the period. It was about some married couples sleeping around with one another and not much more, if I remember correctly, but in the natural and beautiful setting the film had a lot of appeal. The cinematography and editing were good, for it was slow-moving and thorough and digestible, so that one could involve oneself with the actors. When you look at movies from that era, you notice how slow-paced many are and devoid of foul language as well as lacking in graphic violence, which is so prevalent in today's popular films.

Shortly thereafter I met some people through Buddha who were casters of local TV commercials and bookers of printwork. My portfolio was starting to become presentable. It now contained acceptable figure shots in bathing suits and evening dresses and a few "casual" pictures in jeans and shirts. There was one clownish shot also, where I was dressed in a painter's overall, making a pouty grin. I later learned that in my case anyway all of these different styles of imagery are to not much avail. You are always typecast anyway.

The first commercial I got was modeling swimwear for a department store in New York called Korvettes, and I got my first residual awhile afterward. The advertising agency was at the time called Lois, Holland, Calloway. My next job was a Revlon test commercial through a production company called Tulchin, and the ad agency was Leo Burnett. It was a test only; nevertheless, it felt like quite an achievement. The idea was to get work, and as often as possible.

In one commercial I was in, for Arrow shirts, girls were standing around a good-looking man in a semicircle admiring him and his shirt. No talent required there!

I did another one for a Hannover House Bodytrimmer with some kind of exercise gadget with my legs up in the air. No talent needed there, either, except for gymnastics. On TV my legs appeared for half a second.

A little more acting the next time: They wanted a French accent. It was only when a European accent or look or language was sought that I got some kind of speaking role or principal player part. This was a commercial for Tuffitips Nail Enamel. I did a little speech about "splitting, cracking, and peeling nails—Tuffitips works!" poised on a balcony in Manhattan in front of Union Square, where there was this arch in the background, which gave the appearance of l'Arc de Triomphe in Paris. When I saw the commercial on TV, in the middle of the night no less, I was horrified at how strained I looked. The reason had been the traffic below, which had forced me to speak as loudly as possible.

I got another type of engagement, a so-called Industrial, through Buddha. This was an "in-house" presentation for Bankers' Trust, a new kind of copy machine or whatever it was. The job was quite fun. I was now portraying an assistant to the boss in an office trying to look very competent. The pay at that time was good, a few hundred dollars, SAG scale for half a day's work.

Soon enough I was introduced to a very important casting director, Barbara Clayman. Buddha had many good contacts in the business, not only of the peculiar kind. It was my Valentin head shot as well as a "composite," used at the time, a small foldout with three or four pictures of different looks, that were so well received in that office. So now I was cast in several commercials, one after the other, during the course of the next two years.

Suddenly I got a lot of work, and it was simply due to one good head shot. That was the way it happened for so many models and actors. One single picture could land you a "million jobs," whereas many other tested and tried ones got you nowhere. And then all of a sudden it would all come to a halt. The casting director moved away or quit the business, new people came in, and they wanted new faces.

Through Barbara Clayman I did mostly model-type

commercial spots for Casual Corner Clothing, Right Guard, Dupont, Oomphies Shoes, Diners Club, Coty Perfume, Johnson & Johnson, and Hanes Hose through advertising agencies such as J. Walter Thompson, Benton & Bowles, Kurtz & Tarlow, Compton Adv., Dancer, Fitzgerald & Sample, and others. However, these were not principal player parts. They were SAG background player appearances, I was a SAG extra. Nonetheless, a SAG extra player in a commercial made good money, and such a booking was considered very desirable. You had to audition for it, and the competition was just as fierce as for the principal jobs. You had to be well known to the casting director and/or the production company people. Some actors got a tremendous amount of work that way.

The commercials I worked in were either in a studio or on location. For instance, we were in a sailboat race for a Schlitz beer spot, all day long. It was unbearably hot, summer in New York, and I got sun poisoning on my neck from the relentless sun beating down on me.

Another hot one that I was in was in a very large studio, on 106th Street in Harlem. It was 104 degrees in mid-August, and the air conditioner had to be turned off. This is always the case during filming. The background sound should not be heard. It was a commercial for Marine Midland Bank. My action was to walk past a father and a son who are talking about opening a checking account. The son is not paying attention to his father's advice because he is distracted by me in this figure-hugging blue dress. In that humidity and heat it clung to me, and later I had to peel it off in my perspiration. "Son, you've got some head on your shoulders!" exclaimed the father in the scene. I was almost "upgraded" to principal in this one because of my interaction with the principals. However, I lost my chance due to the fact that my head was cut out of the commercial. Just a body walking by did not justify principal status and accompanying residuals. But it was a good "shoot."

Possibly the best job I ever had in a commercial was one for Sony TV. This was years later. I was playing a medieval lady-in-waiting in a magnificent costume made of brown-and-gold brocade. (These clothes come out of the various wardrobe companies associated with show business.) We were all placed on a platform in a studio. There was the king, the princess, three knights, and all the surrounding players, i.e., the court, which consisted of me, another lady-in-waiting, a lute player, a monk, a jester, other music players, and a Great Dane. There was smoke because the scene had to look dreamlike, I supposed. The knights came to propose to the princess, but only the one with the Sony TV got the girl. It took one whole day to shoot and was very interesting, technically and otherwise. I made a big sum of money, including the fitting time for the costume. These bookings could be very lucrative. You could make a thousand dollars a day.

One commercial I was a principal in was for a fur company. This was a long time ago. Today I would not do such a job due to my opposition to the fur industry. Here they wanted a European look and accent, and there was a little copy, a few lines, to speak. A friend of mine referred me to the casting person, and my friend and I were both in it along with two other actresses. We were made up in such a way with catlike eyes in colors of blue, violet, green, and yellow! I was the green one. We had on a variety of fur coats, all in the summer heat once more. We worked in several scenes, of which one was on an airplane out at JFK Airport of all places! One of my lines was: "We're open Sundays, too!" in a Swedish accent.

9
Book Covers and Lingerie

During my entire time in show business I did very few voice-overs. A voice-over is when you just hear the spokesperson for a product, or it can be a narrator. The face is not on camera, but you are still considered a principal performer in commercials and industrials. Some actors are very successful in this field, and it is one of the hardest areas of show business to break into.

I remember auditioning for a radio commercial in which they wanted a "sexy" Swedish voice describing a candy bar. It was at one of the major advertising agencies. I spoke into a microphone and did as best as I could to sound seductive. They said they loved it. However, an all-American male voice was used instead for that candy bar. Casting people do not always know what they are looking for. In order to do this kind of work legitimately, you had to join AFTRA, the American Federation of Theatre and Radio Artists. It was a little easier than joining the Screen Actors Guild, because once one was in the latter, one could automatically become a member of the former and just had to pay a fee, usually after having performed in any one category.

Another time I was up for a Scandinavian Airlines

radio commercial. It was a pretty good audition, I thought, but I never heard from the casting people again. To my astonishment when I listened to the same voiceover a few months later on radio it sounded just like me! It would have been quite possible in those days to have taped my voice and used it and avoided paying me. I was not a member of AFTRA yet, and there was no way of proving that I had been cheated. When I spoke to Buddha about it, we decided, that there wasn't much we could do.

The next voice-over I ended up doing was for a small company called Cinecontact. This time a German accent was required in order to sound like Marthe Keller in a trailer for the movie Black Sunday, in which she played a terrorist who was threatening to bomb a major sports arena in the USA in the name of some kind of cause. I started speaking into the microphone: "People of America!" and then went on and on from the script, an ominous rhetoric, for a full two hours. It was good experience; that was all. The pay was not scale, but after that I could certainly join AFTRA.

Another side of the business was the industrials. I have done a handful of them spread out over twenty years or so. One was a so-called promo film, in which another actor and I played the leads for a miniseries on CBS, an enactment of a steamy novel titled *Scruples*. It was a twenty-second scene out of the novel where I, dressed in a negligee (!), am going to seduce my boss in a hotel room. In the first shot I look in the mirror, contemplating my action, and then proceed toward his room. He opens the door and gives me a look of astonished pleasure. I glide past him in the doorway with a slight flick of my head while the narrator continues, "Billie knew what she wanted, and nothing would stop her. . . . She would pursue all ends . . . to get what she wanted. . . ." The model/woman Billie on the book cover did not look like me at all!

Soon enough I would be modeling for book covers myself. It was those sexy, steamy novels, the so-called Gothic romance novels. Now hereced was something I really would enjoy doing, these new bookings, and I made a slew of them. I have a collection of the book covers and pictures of me and other models, male and female, in conjunction with those photography sessions. The picture on the front cover of this book is one of the studio shots. The photographer was Bob Osonitch who specialized in this type of work. He was introduced to me by Buddha also. Bob was one of the kindest, most professional, soft-spoken, and gentle people I ever met in the business. There was never any fuss or stress around him. It was a pleasure to work with such a mild-mannered man, and what was also so beneficial was that you could *act* in these little scenario shots.

The way it worked: He took a lot of pictures, several rolls of film of the model/actors in various dramatic staged setups in his studio, and then an illustrator would take over and draw the images from the photographs, the end result that you see on the book covers. His studio was located off 14th Street on the Lower East Side. You walked up a few stairs. It was quite a seedy old building, like so many others where you moved around town, going on auditions and go-sees. Often you had to travel to rather unsafe areas in the city, but you soon got used to it. There was a thrill to it. You could always play the starving actress part, not looking too affluent. Mostly you wore black anyway, just like today in New York.

So, for a while I did a lot of book cover bookings for Bob Osonitch. It paid thirty-five dollars an hour, not so bad on those days for money on the side. Those novels were a source of great amusement. For example, the words on the covers: *The Reluctant Adventuress,* a romantic adventure novel, where I and an elegant gentleman from England's Regency era are looking into each other's eyes. We were dressed in period clothes, and Bob Osonitch took a lot of shots of us acting in dramatic poses and displaying emotions. Another one was called *The Encounter,* with a man kneeling and kissing my hand in a mountain lodge. This particular actor, by the way, was very busy all the time, appearing in films, TV, and printwork. He had a look that really was "marketable." There was another book called *The Nude Who Never* with me looking into the camera draped in black satin, off the shoulders, with the text alongside: "She's wildly innocent, innocently sexy and sexually wild!" What drivel! Sometimes it was hard work sitting on the floor like that, posing for a long time holding the same position. And another one: "She was beautiful, she was ruthless, and she hated men." Here I was the one who was kneeling in front of a man, dressed as a maid, no less, and looking not so ruthless at all!

I was a nurse on *Lake Resort Nurse,* and on *The Ghost and the Garnet* I portray a lady of the manor looking a little more evil. Bob Osonitch would tell us the story line of the novel, whereupon we created the look together. It was fun.

Once in a while we did some nudity, twice for Bob, which was OK. One such job was a book cover called *The Goss Women.* It was a picture of the three of us women. One was a friend of Buddha, a successful and beautiful actress whom I will call Annette, who also was very funny, witty, and lively. She was totally comfortable in the nude. We did this job together, a piece of cake.

The other time was for *Playboy* magazine. No, it was

not at all a nude glamour shot. It was to be an illustration for an article about—guess what?—the female orgasm! I was happy to oblige.

When I saw the *Playboy* issue, there was just this drawing of my body, and again I had no head! It was cropped, thank God, and the rest of me was altered a little, and there were all these arrows pointing at different parts of the figure for the purpose of demonstrations in this "scientific" study.

Other bookings I did in the early seventies were lingerie jobs. I did very little high fashion or cosmetic shots because, as I stated, my face was not model material. The only one I came close to was the Revlon test commercial.

I did some hosiery catalog print shots. You were paid $120 an hour for that, so it was quite sought after. It was hard work. You had to keep the same position for several minutes, sometimes holding your breath, and keep the stomach very flat. Maybe you had to sit on the floor in an awkward position or lean into a chair backward.

I did one bra ad. It did not appeal to me very much. A friend of mine, who was in the business as well, was up for this particular job also. It was through a print agency we both worked with. I got the booking. The bra was Playtex and a little pointed, a little stiff. This little event turned into a joke over the years. My friend has a lively sense of humor, and she would from time to time remind me that I got the bra job or "the job of the pointed bra" instead of her, because I must have had a pointed chest!

Other print jobs I did were, for instance, ads for medicine in medical journals. In one ad I was a very sick girl suffering from some kind of mysterious female disease, and I am looking very uncomfortable and miserable in a hospital gown.

The time had now come for another phase in my "career." Enough already with lingerie sessions and posing for photographers. Around the same time I started working in films. It was going to be hundreds and hundreds of them over a period of thirty years. There would be good shoots and bad ones and sometimes ugly ones, but all quite worthwhile.

Buddha said there were three reasons to work in show business, even if you never made it to stardom: one, income, second, the pure enjoyment of it; and third, after ten years you qualified for a pension and, depending on the circumstances, medical insurance.

10
Sylvia Fay—Casting Director of the Upscale

I will never forget the first meeting I had with Sylvia Fay. Buddha, whenever he spoke to her on the phone in his little cubicle apartment on 57th Street, used to cry out with delight, *Sylvia!* and then, "I'll send her right over; she is a good talent. . . . Yes, of course, Sylvia . . . anything you say. . . . Yes, Sylvia . . . of course, I understand. . . ." Ms. Fay had a possibly tolerable relationship with Buddha, putting up with his charades and willing to interview some of his protegée model/actresses. She probably thought of him with mild amusement, and she always had a lot of work for "the girls." She was and still is one of the biggest casting directors of minor film work in New York, i.e., so-called background work and bit parts, special ability parts, stand-in work, and, for some lucky few, principal roles now and then. These were major features shot in the New York area, and they were always Screen Actors Guild signatories. When you worked for Sylvia, you knew it was a legitimate booking, and everything from her casting calls, to showing up for work, to dressing correctly for the part, to everyone's behavior on the set as well as in the "holding area," where the actors were waiting between the takes, was very organized, disciplined, and professional. Sylvia Fay was very strict.

The first time I met her was a little different, though, for me. It was in 1971 and not the usual kind of audition with Sylvia Fay. This was an interview with a producer/director for a film to be shot in New York, and it turned out to be quite an uncomfortable surprise.

Sylvia was present as an "introducer." She was attractive, very blond, short and slim, well dressed, and very businesslike: "Go upstairs and see him. He is waiting for you now."

I remember the place to be a hotel room. The man was there and maybe someone else in the background. To my horror, the role required a nude scene, which fact had not been clearly explained to me. I was not thrilled at all, but being new to the business and especially to Sylvia Fay, I thought it not wise to back away at that moment. So, just like it was done in a movie "wardrobe" area, I undressed in the bathroom and wrapped a towel around me. This producer apparently had already seen a number of girls before me, and perhaps it was not so much of an issue—they needed a body in a movie scene; it could have been a "double" for a principal actress. It was a real audition, although embarrassing. I removed the towel. He took one polite look and said the usual, "Thank you," and, "Good-bye." That was all; however, in the future I promised myself never to disrobe again.

As for Sylvia Fay, I developed the best relationship with her. I would be working for her in hundreds of movies during the next three decades, and all of those jobs in films eventually led to my securing a SAG pension. There were other casting directors and other film work also of course contributing to the pension, but from her I got the bulk of the credits.

Sylvia was accompanied by Fleet Emerson, her right-hand man and co-caster, a very gentle and professional person, who would patiently describe to you in detail how you were supposed to be dressed for a particular shoot: "Aimée, they want a very upscale cocktail dress, no blue, no red, no bright colors, no white, and preferably no black—we already have too much black. Do you have something in a muted tone? Wine red is OK or dove gray. Lots of jewelry and matching accessories. Bring two or three upscale wardrobes [you usually got paid to bring extra sets of clothes]. Your hair has to be made up in curlers, so it can be combed out on set, and you must do your own makeup." This was upscale background work, and the *look* was very important, especially the colors, in view of the film's lighting and so forth.

Sylvia Fay did not like bare arms for women over thirty-five. Arms lose their muscle tone, and the camera could possibly exaggerate the appearance thereof. When working on a film, in the so called holding area, where all the players assembled during the intervals between the shooting of the scenes (unless you were staying in a camper, if you had a bit part or otherwise), Sylvia would hold little speeches about what was acceptable behavior and what was not, like arriving too late in the morning, not having the appropriate wardrobe, asking too many unnecessary questions, complaining about the working conditions, or generally creating a nuisance or being a pest. Smoking! God forbid! Don't even think about it. So if your arms were bare and you were "average" could you please get a coverup from the wardrobe department? This was an important and powerful entity that could make or break "your look." It was never your own look; it was the look required for the film. You had no business pleasing yourself, looking attractive in *real* life. Your "role" was to fit the scene. For instance, lots of powder was required on the face in order to eradicate shine, which would look ghastly in daylight. The clothes they gave you to wear, especially for period films, could be very uncomfortable or torturous, as I will describe later.

Sylvia Fay used to comment on my high-heeled shoes. My roommate at that time was also in the business. When Fleet told her what to wear over the phone, you could hear Sylvia in the background calling out, "Tell her to borrow Aimée's shoes. *Stewardesses* always wear *high-heeled shoes!*" and we would be laughing up a storm. "Oh, those high-heeled shoes," Sylvia used to say to me, looking me up and down. Then she called me Emela. "I gotta say, that's a nice dress!" She favored designer clothing. I had a few outfits in that department, but more often than not, the clothes I wore in the "upscale" scenes just looked like they were but had been bought in outlet stores on 34th Street. Once, when I looked "grand dame"–ish for some reason and Sylvia happened to peek inside the holding area, she gave me a long look and exclaimed, "Madame Bratt!" The whole room exploded with laughter.

In the movie *Moonstruck,* the famous line by Sylvia will not be forgotten. The male background players dressed in formal wear, were placing rubber covers over their shoes in the wet weather outside the Met in New York. You could hear Sylvia loud and clear: "I don't want any rubbers!"

In the film *Cocktail,* in which my roommate and I worked, it was supposed to be a very glamorous scene. Sarah (not her real name) had brought a pretty outfit, however, it was not up to Sylvia's standards. The wardrobe department transformed Sarah with a shocking pink organza dream of a dress. "Now that's what I want!" Sylvia stated emphatically.

Also, as regards Sarah, one day when she ran into Sylvia on the street after having been absent for quite a while from the business, Sylvia invited her to reregister in her office on Park Avenue and when pulling out her file exclaimed, "Oh yes, you're the pain in the ass who does not like to work in smoke!" At the time a less toxic although not entirely harmless kind of smoke was used on movie sets.

There were many more anecdotes about Sylvia Fay. She is a famous lady in the business, feared by some, admired by many. She takes no nonsense from anyone, including the people she deals with in the industry. That is her reputation, anyway. Even outside show business, she would not hesitate to use her authority. Once, when I worked in the film *All That Jazz*, I had been summoned to appear in court. It was my own case. However, Sylvia protested matter-of-factly, "I'll get you out of court! I can absolutely not replace you!" Thank you, Sylvia. Needless to say, the "show must go on," and it did. No court case.

The films I did background player work in through Sylvia Fay were, as I have said, hundreds, starting in 1971 into the present time. Just a few examples: *The Bell Jar, Oliver's Story, The Sentinel, All That Jazz, Raging Bull, The Fan, The World according to Garp, Death Wish, Still of the Night, Wall Street, Baby Boom, Goodfellas, First Wives Club,* and features for TV: *The Dain Curse, Prisoner without a Name, Cell without a Number, Izzy and Moe, Charles & Diana, a Royal Romance,* and many, many more, as well as television series such as *The Equalizer,* in which I worked at least fifteen times, *Kojak,* and Law and Order, in which I worked at least twenty-five times.

Following are my memories of some New York–made features cast by Sylvia Fay.

On the Set of *Raging Bull*

When Fleet called me, he said, "You will be a cigarette girl! Go to Fifty-fourth Street for the fitting. It's a four-day booking or possibly longer, and they will require you to put your hair in pincurls, so they can coif you according to the period, the nineteen-forties. They will do the makeup. Call me back on Monday for the call time and location between four and five in the afternoon. Thank you, Aimée."

Raging Bull was to become the best critically acclaimed film of the seventies, a wonderful portrayal of the life of the middleweight champion Jake La Motta from the Bronx, starring Robert De Niro and Joe Pesci. De Niro, as you recall, got the Oscar for his role.

Working in this film was possibly the best and most exciting job I ever had in show business. Jake La Motta himself was present and hung around the set, coming and going. He looked a little smug, a hulking figure, still looking a bit like the Bull. Martin Scorcese, the awe-inspiring director, had a whole entourage around him. Smoking was forbidden anywhere near him. I have worked in several Scorcese films: *Goodfellas, Age of Innocence, Taxidriver.* There is always a bit of mystery, anticipation, and magic on his film sets. Everybody is at attention in the presence of his excellence. He is like quicksilver, with penetrating eyes and rapid movements.

The scene I was going to appear in was in a restaurant next to the Plaza on 60th Street, which was transformed into the famous old Copacabana nightclub of the forties, The Copa. If you have seen the movie, it is the Copa scene where Jake La Motta (De Niro) is being lauded and honored as "the Raging Bull from the Bronx" and then later a fight ensues. I am walking around in both scenes all dressed up as a forties cigarette girl in a little short dress, fishnet stockings, high-heeled shoes, a giant cigarette tray with a sling around my neck, my hair swept up in big locks with red cherries in it. I had red, red lipstick, rouged cheeks, and so on. The shot opens up with all the people at the tables and me in the middle, walking around with my cigarette tray from customer to customer pausing here and there. The takes of two scenes lasted four days. The makeup and hair sessions were an ordeal. There were many women, most of them restaurant patrons, sitting at the bar and the numerous tables, who had to be coiffed and made up forties style, and whenever you work in a period movie that part is very, very time-consuming. Tempers can flare. It is very crowded and can be very hot, and what the stylists do to your hair, teasing, curling with hot irons, pulling and twisting, sometimes coloring, sometimes putting ugly wigs on your head, is not a pleasant experience. And then the makeup! Period makeup can look hideous. There is pancake powder, (around the eyes, too), scarlet red lipstick. It gets interesting, when you are made up to look ashen pale or dead (!) or look scary and disturbed, like I did in a bit part in a movie called *Presumed Innocent,* or completely covered with white paint like in *All That Jazz.*

In *Raging Bull* I enjoyed being this perky-looking cigarette girl with all the cherries. I had a great deal of fun on that shoot. The actresses I was working with, another cigarette girl and a friend of hers, got us together with all kinds of people associated with Scorcese who were either in the film or from the outside. They took us to lunch and dinner every single day and evening. These were eighteen-hour days! For lunch we had martinis; for dinner we had champagne! The food was fantastic. All we did between takes was party. At the end of the shoot I needed a lot of sleep.

Still of the Night—The Silent Bit

The phone call from Fleet again: "Aimée, you are going to be, let's see, an auction assistant! You will be working alongside Meryl Streep and two other auction assistants in an auction scene à la Christie's in a location next to Columbia University. Do you have a long dark skirt with a white blouse? It will be shooting for a week or so."

"Yes," I said, "I have a very wide and long pleated navy skirt and white blouse." I also knew that in order to take the time off from my flying job I had to remaneuver my schedule with Pan Am. It was always a challenge to "rearrange" my time. It meant making a dozen or so phone calls, pleading with people (in the airline business) and praying that everything would fall in place schedulingwise. I did not want to give up, let's say, an important Tokyo trip worth many hours as well as a rewarding layover there with shopping, Japanese Shabu Shabu, massage and hair treatments, and other pleasures, and on the other hand I had no intention of rejecting such a lucrative and promising job in this particular film, especially when called by Sylvia Fay. You just did not say no to *her*. Whenever I had to do that because of flying or major fatigue after a flight, I felt uncomfortable. I received a lot of extra income through her, and besides, I liked the orderliness of her calls. There were other casting directors I had no problem saying no to, depending on the type of booking of course. It was not always worth it to change my flights just to make room for a hundred-dollar-a-day walk-on extra job in the street! However, many times I would accept those "bad jobs" in order to earn enough money toward the pension and medical credits. I would say that out of all the calls I got to work in films and TV (not commercials) during thirty years, I had to reject at least one-quarter of them because of my flying schedule and/or the crushing jet lag fatigue following these international trips. I was always very tired on the set. Those early mornings! I was so sleep-deprived at times that I could have lain down in the street and slept on a stone pillow. I would lean against walls and close my eyes between takes and slouch against movie equipment (!), my body aching from lack of rest. Sylvia once saw me lying on the floor in a holding area (I was not the only one, by the way!) and said, "Aaaimée, wake up." But she could not know what shape I was in. Today I could never fly for several days and then walk onto a movie set and work fifteen hours, having to look good as well, never mind staying awake. But I sure managed to do just that for up to thirty years.

Still of the Night was a wonderful job, no matter how tired I was. We were silent bit players, and therefore we got a special holding area, a roomy room with sofas and comfortable chairs and always a table with good food available. "We" were the three auction assistants, a few actor/cops (they were also real cops), the auctioneer (who had a part), the bookkeeper, and a few art assistants in the scene, who carried paintings. We were "upgraded" to bit player status because of our prominent placement or instrumental action in the scene next to the leading Meryl Streep, who played an auction seller in this thriller with Roy Scheider, directed by Robert Benton. I became friendly with my coplayers, especially one of the cops, and had a real good time.

The scene was a very long ongoing one, in which Roy Scheider sits among the multitude of bidders and/or the audience while Meryl Streep is working on the telephone with a client from Italy, who is bidding on the various paintings that are being presented, one after the other. Our action was to behave like assistants with pens and programs following the auction, reacting to this and that, some close-ups now and then, until all of a sudden the star disappears and the mystery unfolds further in the film. It took up to a week to shoot this scene. During my lunch hour I got the maddening idea of taking a taxi all the way to my home in Murray Hill in heavy traffic. Twenty minutes down and twenty minutes back, ten minutes to eat and make phone calls, all in my wide floor-length skirt, dashing like a madwoman in the streets looking for the cabs as well. I had enlisted a friend to drive me back and forth the last day, who instead turned out to be an enemy, because he would not do it without monetary compensation! However, it was a matter of such importance to me that I gave in to his audacity. Many times on these movie shoots I would take a taxi in the middle of the day to transport myself to another location all dressed up in an evening gown or period clothing (subject to the situation) or made up as a character in some other era. People in Manhattan would not even blink, maybe throw me a glance and simply determine that I was just another crazy-looking out-of-date weirdo. "Has the woman no taste?!" I got a little better treatment from the cabdrivers, but only when I told them the reasons for my outfits or nervous behavior, always worried about being late for the next scene after lunch. If you had been "established in the scene" as a player and then were absent suddenly when it came time to shoot, you could be fined under certain circumstances.

The Sentinel—Horror in a Horror Film

One of the very first jobs in show business I had stands out as the most bizarre two weeks of stand-in work. Sylvia Fay had asked if I could be available for this period, standing in for Deborah Raffin in this horror flick with a cast of Sylvia Miles and John Carradine as well as Ava Gardner, directed by a British director. He had a reputation. Known for his skill in making commercially successful films, he was also infamous for behaving at times intolerantly toward his entourage. He appeared pompous and abrasive. However, I was told years later he meant no harm at all and merely exhibited a sardonic sense of humor.

To be a so-called stand-in you had to be roughly the same height and weight and have similar hair color to the person you were standing in for. This is off-camera work, and you are there for the purpose of lighting and camera distance when the scene is set up. Sometimes you will also read the lines in the script and do the whole scene with another stand-in, which gets a little more involved, and your skills come into play somewhat. I have done that a few times, once reading the dialogue of the part of a Swedish housekeeper in the series *Law and Order,* standing in for a Swedish actress. You can also perform as a double, which is on camera, when you have to look like the principal player from behind or sideways perhaps or far away in the distance.

This time, I was standing in, together with another actress, Carolyn, who stood in for Christina Raines, the star of the film. Now Deborah Raffin was a whole head taller than me, but it apparently did not matter in this film. We spent two weeks on this shoot far out somewhere on Long Island. The country was beautiful, the weather wonderful, the food that was served superb, and most of the people we worked with very kind and certainly easygoing out there in the woods, except for the aforementioned director. Well, let's say his bark was worse than his bite. There was also a rather harried script lady, who seemed to display a little contempt for us "extra" stand-ins. She made remarks over trivial issues. Were we always in the way?

I don't like stand-in work for that very reason actually. You feel that you are in the way between takes. Many times on *Law and Order*, for example, where conditions can be very cramped in the studios, there is little room to stand or hide. You must be at your position immediately when called and then quickly disappear afterward into nowhere. I feel like a nonentity or a shadow of the person I am standing in for. However, some actors are very good at this skill. To be a good stand-in requires a lot of work and experience. Some make a good living out of it and work as doubles as well throughout the entire shooting schedule of the film or TV series.

If you ever saw this horror film *The Sentinel*, you know how hideous the scenes are. It is quite good, actually. The director should get credit for that as well as all the other films he made. But his behavior toward his assistants? I was told different stories. He fired one after the other. They would stand by him and wipe his brow when he got hot, as if he were some kind of medieval despot surrounded by attendants. He fired out demands, sometimes a trifle disrespectfully or maybe humorously intended, for example, once about a production assistant: "Tell that bitch to . . ." whatever it was. Carolyn and I would lie in the grass waiting for the next call, "Second Team!" That was the order to go where the camera was and stand in. It was very boring work, long hours of doing absolutely nothing, just standing there. It was better to stay away from the set, because whenever we approached the action there was some kind of stir around the director. In the mornings he would step out of his limousine with script in hand, like some kind of dignitary, three "assistants" in tow, and start barking out orders in his British accent. He shouted at me once, "Stand *there! No, no,* for heaven's sake, *stand there!*"

Thank you! Enough standing for three weeks.

All That Jazz—a Fantasy in a Dream Sequence

Some fantastic job this one! It was scheduled originally for only four days. It turned into two whole weeks. Sylvia Fay had to make a special announcement in the holding area to all of the background players, maybe a hundred of them, to do their best in order to reschedule their availability. These were established scenes, and it was difficult to replace people who could not stay the entire time. That was the occasion when she told me, "I'll get you out of court!" Most of the actors were happy to stay and be a part of this fascinating scene in the film *All That Jazz,* directed by Bob Fosse and starring Roy Scheider, Ann Reinking, Ben Vereen, and others, as well as a minor part by Jessica Lange, whom I ended up standing in for, at the very end of the film. It was the autobiographical story of Bob Fosse himself, and ultimately his heart attack, including a description of the heart operation itself and especially his toying with death and the obsession with it. This "death wish" is incorporated into a magnificent display of a Broadwaylike performance by Ann Reinking, Ben Vereen, and other artists in a special kind of "dream sequence," in which Roy Scheider plays Fosse himself, dancing and singing. This was all taking place in Purchase, New York, on a special stage set up for the film. We, the background players, were the "audience" in this dream sequence, all of us dressed in black, tuxedos and cocktail dresses mostly, and some of us had our faces painted chalky white, in order to make us look more dreamlike and mysterious. Apparently, we were or had been all the people in Fosse's life. There were also a few actors who were painted like eerie silvery statuettes lighted from within, as well as individual characters out of Fosse's life, some made out as caricatures in the dream, nude women and clowns.

My face was painted white every single morning. It was a relief not to have to bother with my own makeup for a while. I had on the same black crepe dress for the two weeks, and my hair was pulled back tightly and tied into an elevated ponytail. After it was over, I threw the dress away, as I often did with other outfits worn during extended movie shoots, as I got so sick of looking at them and wearing them day in and day out.

I was sitting in the "audience." We were all placed on these benches, like in a stadium. The hall was always dark, and there were at least a hundred extra players all in black encircling the stage. Ben Vereen was prancing and singing into the microphone, "I think he's gonna die, I think he's gonna die. . . ." while Ann Reinking and another dancer (I forgot her name) were doing a beautiful jazzy routine dressed in glamourous leotards designed with arteries and veins, representing, or course, Fosse's heart condition. Roy Scheider was in the midst of this singing, "I think I'm gonna die . . . ," while the dancers were caressing him with their arms. "Bye-bye, my life, good-bye . . . bye-bye, happiness . . . hello, loneliness . . . I think I'm gonna die . . ." and then he slides onto the floor in a kind of a finale. At one point we lit candles under our faces and then extinguished them all at once, as part of the choreography.

For two weeks I was sitting on that bench, rehearsing our actions over and over, however minimal, while all different angles were shot. I would readjust my makeup (that was before they painted my face) a little too often, so the man next to me finally blurted out, "I thought that compact would break!"

After that job was over, I was asked a few weeks later if I could come back to be a stand-in for Jessica Lange when she played the Angel of Death at the end of the film. They draped me in a big white sheet while they worked the lights and measured the distances. This one was an enjoyable stand-in job. For months afterward I would be humming the tune "Bye-bye, happiness . . . I think he's gonna die. . . ."

How to choose a head shot

Different styles of photographers' headshots

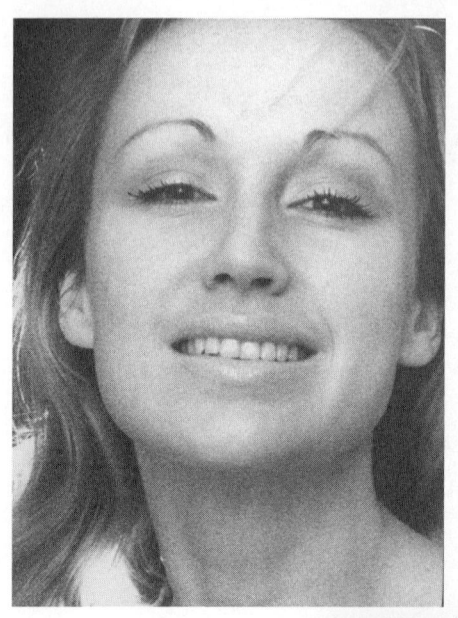

Model poses from the early seventies.

Bookcover print work

From the movie, *Devil's Advocate*

Sony TV Commercial

From *Presumed Innocent*

From *All that Jazz*

Period Film Costumes

From *Arthur*

From *Izzy and Moe*

From *Cradle Will Rock*

From *Age of Innocence*

From *Cradle Will Rock*

From *House on Carroll Street*

From *Pollock*

From *That's Adequate* (TV)

From *Secret of Joe Gould*

From *How to Pick Up Girls*

From *See No Evil, Hear No Evil*

Richard Dubois

Natalie Deutz

Penny Gaston

Nolan Carley

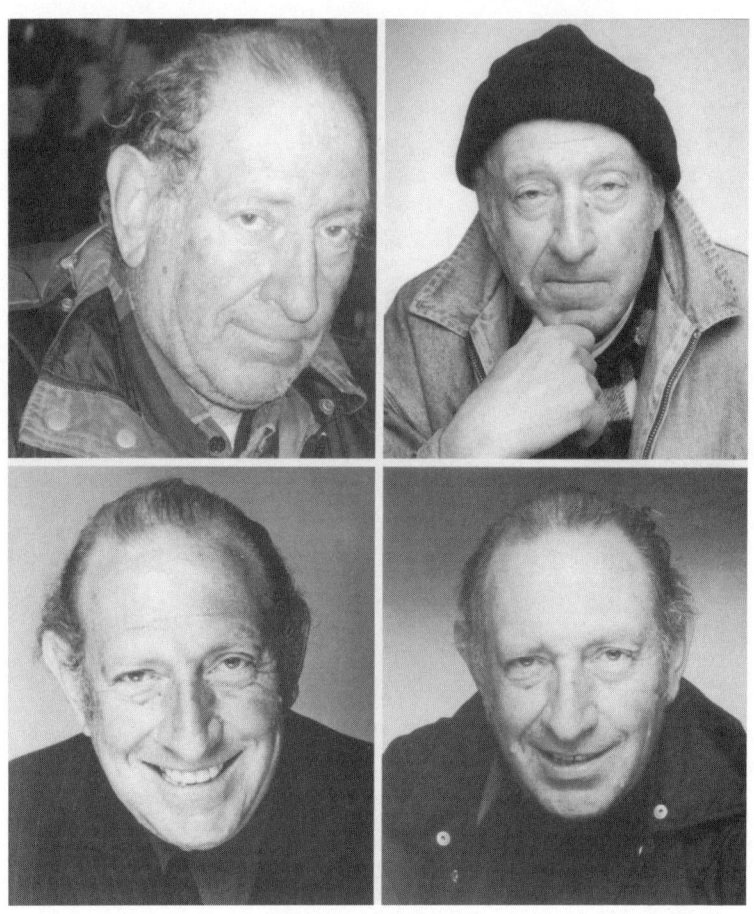

Bernie Friedman

11
The Agony of Being an Extra

It really was a case of the good jobs, the bad jobs, and the ugliest jobs. The good ones were the silent bits, the special ability parts, the upgrades on the set, the scripted parts without speaking lines, and the background work in TV commercials and industrials.

The bad ones, or the so-so ones, were walk-ons in the street, crowd scenes of all varieties, especially in which SAG background actors would be mixed in with nonunion extras, some of them behaving very unprofessionally, chattering in loud voices, making remarks about the ongoing filming, giggling like high school kids or, worst of all, trying to ask for autographs of the stars! Those were the times you wanted to take flight somewhere, and like one actor exclaimed, "They make *me* look bad!" Other bad ones were the excessively drawn-out long hour shoots, which required up to thirty or so retakes, in which you could be standing on the set in high-heel shoes for hours, waiting between the camera setups and lighting adjustments. It would be so boring and fatiguing and painful to stand up like that, sometimes all night long with only ten-minute breaks far and few in between. In the film *Great Expectations* it was just like that, although it was a very beautiful set in colors of emerald green with gold and black tuxedos worn by the men. Unfortunately, much of this sparkle and glitter is lost in the film itself, a fact that is very often the case in films. You have these magnificent, elaborate sets and all the labor behind them, and in the final version of the film all you see is a few seconds of the same and sometimes just a blur.

Also among the bad ones were those when you were treated shoddily: overly cramped quarters in the holding area, not enough chairs to sit on, temperature settings from ice-cold to hot and unhealthy, inadequate catering or tasteless junk food on the tables in the holding area (not to be confused with lunch and dinner breaks). Now and then one could be subjected to a nasty PA (production assistant) or AD (assistant director) or rude wardrobe people and nervous or snappy makeup and hair people. Note: I don't see that so much anymore! The actors themselves could be *bad*. And some of the crew! Why so much talk! And the loudness! "Quiet on the set!" someone would yell, but the talking continued. "*Quiet!*" the director would roar in exasperation. See, Americans are a friendly bunch, and we love to have conversations. If it was in Sweden, nobody would say "Boo!" Over there it is so quiet, you think something must be wrong. Oppressive, at times.

If you are a member of the Screen Actors Guild, it means that you are officially an actor or player, whether you do principal work or background work, hence the contract terms *background player* and SAG *extra player*, or as of today, *background actor*. In order to join the guild you must have been a "principal on camera" in either a film or commercial or industrial that is a signatory of the guild. You are now legitimately in the "business of acting" and serious about it, not hired off the street as a nonentity, or someone who is not associated with show business. I think, therefore, on most sets one is treated acceptably well. At least in New York, it is well known, that many actors have done or are doing both principal and extra work (there is no Extras' Guild like in California) and are respected for it accordingly. Some may disagree.

Why would an actor bother with extra work? Simple answer: to make a living. Actors do not earn that much unless they are very successful, but the industry needs them nonetheless. According to SAG information some years ago, 80 percent do not make a living wage. It used to be ninety percent made under $10,000 a year.

Now to the ugliest jobs: Ugh, how would you like to stand for a half-day on a snowy mound in the middle of winter in degrees of minus twenty Centigrade and not be allowed to leave the spot until shooting was over? Talk about jeopardizing your health! The film was *The Super,* starring Joe Pesci. I am sure he is a considerate individual, who would never know that a hundred feet from him and the main action, a few people were suffering in hell. Short of frostbite we were stamping our feet into the ground and clapping our gloved hands in a frenzy. I looked at the dogs, who were romping around happily in the snow, and became jealous—of their *fur!* We were dressed in overcoats and thermal underwear and gloves and caps, clothes that can only keep you warm for a limited amount of time, until the inevitable effects of exposure hit you. I almost walked away from the set. This was fifteen years ago. Were it today, I would not have hesitated to walk right over to the AD and protest and threaten action. Upon receiving bookings, there is still sometimes no satisfactory information as to the conditions of the film location environment.

I think before you accept a job it is reasonable to demand an approximate answer as to what kind of circumstances you will be working in: inside or outside, the weather (rain or snow or heat), and the approximate duration of the call. Some of these questions cannot be answered by the casting director, but it still helps if they are willing to share a little information, if they have some idea of, for example, how long the previous days' shooting have been running on a particular film. As for me, I will no longer accept a job that will jeopardize my health. Too many times in the past I accepted jobs when I was advised by the casting person: "It's an inside shot, but bring a coat just in case." When it came time to shoot, 95 percent of the day was spent outside in freezing rain or cold on icy pavements in thin high-heeled shoes (which was part of the wardrobe look). One time my toe ended up bleeding from the hard ice. I contemplated leaving the set and complaining to SAG, but more often than not you decided against it. Who wants to be a troublemaker? And there's the "they'll never use you again!" syndrome.

One of the worst jobs I ever had was in a film made out in the Hamptons called *Dying for Love*. We were transported in buses to and fro. These buses often served as dressing rooms cum sleeping areas cum holding areas. Can you imagine up to fifty people changing clothes in this situation along with all their garment bags and suitcases, women among men in various stages of undress? A sense of humor did not help. It was so unbearably crowded. The toilet in the back of the bus was the only facility available to us for many hours. So you would think that the actors had the sense to keep it as clean as possible. Someone came out of there once and yelled, "Who had the nerve to pee all over the seat!" It turned out to be more embarrassing than intended. One man, whether he was the offender or not, showed a little too much reaction and muttered something in irritation.

When we arrived, the location was inside as well as outside a very beautiful Hampton house. A few of us, two couples, were placed out on the lawn. It was some kind of garden party, and we were the guests. My friend Sarah was there, and we were coupled with our "dates." All night long! We froze! It was April, but in the film it was supposed to be summer. We had light summer dresses on, and the temperature dropped into the forties. I thought I was going to die! Between the endless takes we had jackets to put on, but the jackets had to come off as soon as they were ready to shoot. "Jacket off!" the damnable AD would shout at the top of his lungs, because he was far away. This was a wide shot, and they were *never* ready to shoot. Several minutes would pass, exposing us further to the cold. "Jackets off!" "Jackets on!" Our bodies had started to shake, at first just a little and then quite violently. It was torture! Never again. It was very bad for an old man, who got so sick that an ambulance had to be summoned. The next day my rib cage was sore from all the shivering and shaking. Half the night we had spent out there on the lawn.

Another cold day, thirty years ago, in the movie *Hair*, one of my first jobs ever, we, hundreds of extras, were placed in the Wall Street area, where we had to do some kind of choreographed mass movement, sitting, standing, and turning at the same time. It looks good on film, but it was an awful experience. The only bright point about it was that I made the acquaintance of a certain individual by the name of Bernie Friedman, a Runyonesque character actor, of whom I will write more in a later chapter. He made me laugh the entire day, carrying on in his Bronx jargon, so I felt warmer in the icy wind.

Other "ugly" jobs included situations in which you were forced to stand in the street for hours, sometimes in evening gowns, very uncomfortable, waiting for the director to make up his mind when to start shooting; the ADs called you to the set much too early, because general terms could not be agreed upon; or there was an unnecessary lack of communication or tense or unpleasant conditions on the set. Some film shoots got a reputation after a little while and were best to be avoided.

12
The Joy of the Upgrade

To be upgraded on the set is a feeling of minor success. You were hired as a background player, and then for any one reason, whether it be your look, the way you were dressed, or even if you have been given a little interaction with a leading actor in a scene, however fleetingly, you could be elevated to "silent bit" status. It could be some action like bumping into the star, for example, or a reaction shot or any other kind of special performance relevant to the story line, which would be considered "furthering the plot," either out of the script or not at all. You could be given a line to speak and then upgraded to "dayplayer" status.

It was often a matter of chance or luck. Sometimes, however, if you volunteered to speak a few words that would not automatically qualify you as a dayplayer. Also, if you spoke a line, the microphone may not have been directly above you, or the words were just part of the background murmur or an "omni," in which several actors talked. It can be a very gray area.

If you were hired to dance the tango or play the piano or do skateboarding or perform some special skill, you would get "special ability" credit and the higher pay for that. Sometimes, simply out of pure courtesy, you could be upgraded for just wearing and appearing in your underwear, or you could be a featured background player, standing out as an individual, like "the bejewelled lady," "the horrified juror," or "the crying housewife," and so on.

Sometime in the early seventies I was cast as a college girl in the film *Bell Jar,* the story about Sylvia Plath, the poet and writer. This was an upgrade, considered "special ability," because we were running in and out of dormitory rooms clad in pretty undergarments. In another film, *Me and Him,* we became silent bit players because again we appeared in underwear in a subway car in the middle of the night, a daydream sexual fantasy scene for the voyeuristic leading man, who was apparently having trouble controlling "him."

In the film *Insignificance,* which was critiqued by one reviewer as "this insignificant movie," I was upgraded to a makeup lady, 1950s style, in a reenactment of the filming of the scene in which Marilyn Monroe is standing on the subway grating in *The Seven Year Itch.* This was a movie within a movie.

In *Secret of My Success* I was a receptionist, who says, "Good Morning!" to Michael J. Fox in an office scene while he is trying to climb the corporate ladder in this film of the eighties. In that one I got silent bit credit, not dayplayer, although I had that one speaking line, but it was hardly worthwhile to create an issue about it.

In *Baby Boom,* around the same time, I was a businesswoman walking down the street and handing a newspaper to a man. We were upgraded (me and others) because we were part of the opening credits, in which the narrator energetically introduces the up-and-coming careerwoman of the eighties: "As little girls we were brought up and told to marry lawyers and doctors . . . but then we *became* lawyers and doctors . . ." and continues on a little patronizing. (I was never *told* to marry a lawyer or doctor when I was a little girl!).

In the suspense-filled drama *Presumed Innocent* I had a scripted silent bit, quite a dramatic one, of which I will relate more later. The reason I was chosen for that little part had a lot to do, I think, with my suit and the drab color of it. I was supposed to be a very disturbed woman. A friend of mine, Penny, was also called for the same character, but she was dressed in red, a happy color.

In some TV shows, when I was upgraded on the set it happened also mostly by chance. In *The Equalizer* I became a gangster's girlfriend, sitting in a bar scene, simply because I was at the right place at the right time. The original actress was absent and arrived too late from lunch. When it came time to shoot, they just asked me to take her place. Perhaps the color of my dress was correct again.

I got another very good upgrade in a TV pilot called *Tattinger's,* starring Jerry Stiller among others, this time also because someone did not show up for work! The right wardrobe was once more the reason, this time for sure. I also had the right "look," inspected and okayed by the director himself. Tattinger's was a restaurant where everything was going wrong, and Jerry Stiller played the owner. We, my husband, who had a speaking part in it, and I, enter the establishment. "We have a reservation!" he says in anticipation, only to be rebuffed by the owner: "Congratulations! Sit at the bar!" We proceed to it. "Only a coupla minutes," he calls out again, striding into the kitchen, where obvious chaos is the order of the day. My hands go up in the air in protest at this mediocre service in the restaurant, whereupon Jerry Stiller points to me and exclaims in an effort to pacify us, the customers, "By the way, *nice dress!*"

13
A Potpourri of Little Film Stories

The following is an account of special memories from film jobs and situations relating to them that stand out over the rest during the course of thirty years, starting in the seventies and up to the present time. I've had over 300 jobs in New York–made features and TV shows and commercials and industrials, not counting at least a hundred more calls I could not accept because of my airline occupation.

Oliver's Story was a film in which I had a walk-on part as a Pan American stewardess (the term used at the time). It was just a one-day job at the airport, but I became friendly with some of the film crew members. After the New York scenes were shot, to my great astonishment, they all walked on board my next Tokyo flight, when I was working as in-flight purser. The director and cameraman and a few others were seated in First Class and the rest of the film crew in Economy. (We never called it Coach.) This was a very long nonstop flight, fourteen hours. Equally surprised at seeing me on the plane, the director delightedly said, "We got a good shot of you in the film!"

Well, "Thank you, hope you enjoy your flight," I said halfheartedly. It now happened that I was not in the best of moods, because Pan Am, having financial difficulties as always was the case then, had shortchanged us with catering and other equipment and as purser I was responsible for cabin procedures and delivery. I could have quite a temper, and the story goes, according to an old friend of mine, Britt Marie who was working with me on the flight, that at one instant in a fit of fury at Pan Am I just dumped a piece of serving equipment on the floor (or "threw a tray," as she put it!) in First Class. Unprofessional in the extreme, yes, and a little shocking, but a lot of irregularities occurred at Pan Am in those days. However, the film crew, I remember distinctly, did not even *blink an eye,* maybe a few guffaws and then back to reading their scripts. They just wanted to arrive in Tokyo on time and get some sleep. Besides, they were used to drama. The rest of the flight proceeded very pleasantly. Later on, when I met some of them on other film shoots, the only comments were: "Oooaah, what a long flight!!!"

As far as working with the stars in all of these New York films, you never ever approached them unless you had some kind of interaction in a scene. Dustin Hoffman was one of the funniest and sweetest actors I came across. In *Kramer versus Kramer,* there was a street scene where I walked past him. "When you walk by me," he turned to me and joked and said offhandedly, "why don't you wiggle a little, so I've got something to look at!" Sure, but it did not qualify as an upgrade. In *Tootsie* I bumped into him and gasped in surprise, somewhere in the dressing area, at seeing him all dressed up as a woman in a corset and wig and with an amused grin on his face.

Lauren Bacall had a sense of humor. In *The Fan* I walked toward the camera in a party scene where people were dancing. I had on a long black skirt with a slit on the side, and when she walked onto the set, she glanced at my skirt and lifted her eyebrows in that characteristic way and smiled approvingly.

In *The World According to Garp* we had to cry. It was a memorial scene with Robin Williams and others. I was placed on a podium in a chair. Someone was making a very emotional speech about the woman who had been murdered. Droplets of oil were placed under our eyes. However, after several takes I began to really cry listening to this actress's moving performance or was it only crocodile tears?

One of the most enjoyable little roles I was ever cast in was as a bridesmaid in the movie *Arthur* with Dudley Moore and Liza Minelli. We were special ability players, six of us, bridesmaids. It was the church scene, in which Dudley, half-drunk, does not want to marry his bride-to-be and the future father-in-law decks him, to the floor. All the bridesmaids dressed up in frilly dresses and hats with lace and ribbons scream in horror. I and one other bridesmaid dash out through the door leading into the pew area from the little vestibule, almost colliding with Liza, who suddenly makes her entrance and now finds Arthur on the floor.

Have you ever seen a cougar in a convertible? It was in the movie *Who's That Girl?*, starring Madonna. My action was to walk in and out of a doorway at Trump Plaza on Fifth Avenue. Well, I did just that a hundred times for several days, and if that was not enough, then came the reshoot at a later date. It must have been a tricky shot with this car screeching to a halt with this beautiful animal inside along with Madonna in the wee hours of the morning (little traffic around). As for me, I made one tidy sum of money on that film, so I did not mind so much walking back and forth like a robot. I never saw so many retakes! Apparently no budget restraints with megastars like that. However boring it was, the cougar was awesome. "He is the same color as your suit, Aimée!" Sylvia Fay exclaimed happily.

In *See No Evil, Hear No Evil* I played a hooker, a sleazy one. I will never forget this flea-bag motel on the New Jersey Turnpike! It was a very funny film with the twosome Richard Pryor and Gene Wilder as part-time crooks. The cops are in pursuit most of the time and finally arrive with big fanfare at this motel, shouting into megaphones: "This is the *police!* Get out of your rooms, you bumkuses!" and we, the four hookers along with the "johns" and in various stages of undress, step hesitatingly out of the rooms on the second floor, one after the other, to be exposed in shame and bewilderment. What was not so amusing was the conditions at this establishment and movie location. The weather first of all was very damp and cold, and the rooms were the filthiest I had ever seen. We were all freezing along with the wardrobe people and hair and makeup people but making the best of it, joking about the situation, for the few days we were there. This motel was a welfare residence. In the room that was allocated to me and my john, the door only being part of the set in the scene, there were leftover cartons with half-eaten food particles, discarded soda bottles in the corners of the room, and a variety of clothes on hangers suspended over chairs and tables and a broom, which we soon were to find out the purpose of. It certainly was not meant for sweeping the floor.

During one of the takes, while we were waiting to exit the room looking disheveled and confused, all of a sudden a giant rat, the size of a small dog, dashed across the floor two feet from where we were standing. Screams, complaints. Shooting halted temporarily! The SAG representative was summoned. A conference was held. No, nothing could be done about the rats. The show had to go on.

Move on to the nineties. One casting director, who used to work for Sylvia Fay and now headed his own office, had put in a casting notice in *Backstage,* one of the trade papers, for a German-speaking couple to act as tourists in a Harlem scene for a film about rap artists. It was called *Fly by Night.* I was hired almost immediately for the shoot as well as an actor with whom I had worked many times. These were supposed to be day player parts, although we never got to speak any lines in the film but got some good exposure. The scene was on Malcolm X Boulevard in Harlem, where two of the principal actors were talking about their exploits, one black guy and one white. Behind them was a cut-out life-size poster of the former president Bush Senior placed on the sidewalk. One of the guys had a dog, a Labrador, who was stretched out lazily lying next to us with a collar around its neck with the inscription "DOG" in huge letters.

"What's his name?" inquires the white guy.

"Well, DOG," replies the black guy, "doggie friend," whereupon we, the tourists from Germany, bend down to pet the dog. The black guy wants to take our picture for two dollars. There is another couple also, older, and he tells them to "butt out" after photographing them also and getting his fee. They quickly disappear. "Hey, Khayyam [name of the white guy], watch!" and he proceeds to perform a lewd act on the poster of Bush. We, the Germans, watch in shock and amazement. It was not a bad scene, and between the takes I wandered around in the streets a little. Harlem was unfamiliar territory, and I was a bit curious. This was in the early nineties, and not surprisingly, the area gave a desolate impression. The lack of cars on the wide streets, old men sitting in chairs on the sidewalk chatting or playing some kind of games, poverty, and a kind of emptiness permeated the surroundings. Suddenly an old man appeared. He was blind but smiled and asked me if I could accompany him across the street. I took notice of his little dog. I obliged willingly, leading him to the other side of the street, while the dog, who was not exactly a Seeing-eye dog, was dancing and jumping around us. "That's Mindy!" said the old man. I found my way back to the set, quite moved by this little interlude. A sweet little old man with a sweet little dog. Heartwarming, in the middle of Harlem.

"What do you get paid for these film jobs?" I get asked frequently. It's all scale pay, depending on the hours you work and in what category. There is half-time, overtime, night pay, "smoke" pay, "wet" pay, wardrobe allowances, meal penalties, and so on. The least you can make is a little over a hundred dollars for up to eight hours of general background work, but you can make over a thousand dollars a day if you work very long hours or get upgraded, as I have mentioned. There are different rates for film work and commercials and industrials. In one movie I worked only as background player, as an example, and made over $700.00 for the one day. It was *She Devil,* in which we got what is called golden time, when you work way into the wee hours of the morning, over fifteen hours. It is very, very tiresome but desirable for obvious reasons. On some jobs you could make thousands of dollars and get little sleep.

One such film was *Mickey Blue Eyes.* I worked in that one off and on for several weeks, made so much money, but never *once* appeared in the film! That is, I was on camera a few times, but it was totally insignificant, all the way in the background. I spent almost all the time in the holding area just chatting with my friends. This is not unusual at all. There have been people hired for months in certain films who made between twenty and thirty thousand dollars and never were on camera!

The reasons for that could be cancellations in the script or decisions not to shoot certain segments or you run out of time or the director changes his mind. People, nonetheless, were hired and had to be paid according to contracts or SAG rules. In one film, not long ago, called *Joe Gould's Secret,* I had been hired for a small featured part. It was a beautiful period film, of the twenties or thirties. I was outfitted and costumed in this elegant clothing along with a great-looking hat, my hair and makeup applied perfectly according to the period. I was waiting in the camper (labeled: WOMAN) half the day alongside an actor, my escort, in his camper labeled: MAN, and we were never called to the set. They had canceled us out. All that work to acquire the look! All dressed up and no place . . . Money wasted? Not really, not that much.

Perhaps the most dramatic bit part I was ever hired for was in the film *Presumed Innocent* with Harrison Ford, Bonnie Bedelia, Greta Scacci, and other stars. The casting director, Grant Wilfley, has a special eye for casting, it seems. I have had some good luck with him getting principal work, for instance an industrial American Express as well as a lot of film work. When his office calls, it is always something featured, however minor roles, which started to happen in the nineties.

Grant Wilfley knew me for a long time, but the new updated head shot I had given him apparently inspired him to ask me to play a disturbed woman, a child-abusing mother (!), in this film *Presumed Innocent.* He thought my picture looked a little cold or hardened. It's not a bad picture of me, but he had a point. So I reported to the set dressed in this gray/beige outfit, as per the instructions, because those were the desired colors and shades of the entire movie. Now Penny, my friend/actress, who could also pass for an "evil" woman, was dressed in red for some reason. She did not care; she has a lot of credits on her résumé. I was seated there in this courtroom scene with the "father" of the little abused boy and my sleazy lawyer. Greta Scacci played the prosecutor, along with Harrison Ford. I was sitting there for two hours dwelling on dark thoughts, depressed and disturbed and condemned, having put my poor child's head in a vise down in the cellar! I was believing in my own hopelessness, and it showed on my face. The little boy was testifying against me, his mother, with the urging of the prosecutor, Greta Scacci, while Harrison Ford was looking down on me with deep concern and horror—even between the takes, it seemed to me! He was rehearsing and thinking. "My mommy hurt my head; my mommy hurt my head . . ." the little boy repeated heartbreakingly. Following that scene, it took them a whole ten minutes to do the shot of me.

What was gratifying about this film job was that Alan Pakula, the director, came up to me twice, once on the set and another time outside next to the holding area, and told me, "What you did there was really good, really very good!" That made my day.

14
Reading for a Part—Am I Wasting My Time?

Auditions! They can be a lot of fun, even if you end up nowhere. I enjoy auditions. At first. It is a hit-or-miss kind of situation. Quite a gamble. Are you right for the part or not? Am I going to waste my time? Well, even if I am making this effort and going out of my way in order to rearrange my schedule, the learning experience is worthwhile, let's say, 50 percent of the time, even if I don't get the booking.

So, the first call, usually for a commercial or industrial, is like a shot in the dark. However, the painful part occurs when you get that callback. Now it is no longer a lark. Now it is business, and one had better shape up and get this job, because it is so close. Over the years I have not had too many auditions for film roles. If you have a foreign accent, especially a Swedish one, you are unquestioningly quite limited as far as speaking parts go. A Swedish accent is not like a British or Italian or Spanish or Japanese accent, which are much more in demand, character roles and all. It also has to be noted that agents and casting directors do a lot of typecasting and they often hire actors according to their looks. If I can sound like an American from Ohio or am able to do an Italian accent from Italy, I am not going to be hired if I look like a Northern European. As far as Swedish actresses are concerned, they have not done so well in the United States. Ingrid Bergman was a star and Greta Garbo a legend a long time ago, and they started out in their native country. Some fashion models have tried breaking into films but did not really succeed, which may be true for other Europeans also. Even French Catherine Deneuve mentioned once, when asked why she did not work more in the United States, that "American films do not exactly have roles for foreign actors very much at all." Minor roles, too, are certainly not abundant, and therefore auditions are far and few between. I can count on one hand the times I have been called for a so-called Swedish part during the course of thirty years.

One audition was for a Swedish maid in the film about Greta Garbo starring Anne Bancroft. The casting director, Joy Todd, a really nice woman, had me read for this very small part in her office. I don't think I had much competition, but the part nevertheless was given to a British actress. In the film she just answers the door for Anne Bancroft.

Another call I got was in a film about the founder of Kellogg, in which everyone was overweight and working out at some kind of health farm, a period movie about the twenties. I was supposed to be a fat Swedish person, so I declined the offer to audition for that one. However, the casting agent was a wonderful older man, by the name of Hanns Wollters, very well known in the business, who specialized in foreign accents and languages. When I saw the film later, there was not a single scene with anyone resembling a Swedish character, fat or otherwise. Probably ended up on the cutting room floor.

I got an audition, nonspecific if you will, what else, but as a flight attendant in the film *Scent of a Woman* with Al Pacino. They just wanted to take a look at me, but apparently I did not correspond to their image of a flight attendant. Ironically, how many times have I appeared in airline uniforms of all kinds in films? More about that later.

One very interesting part I was up for was in a low-budget film called *Rain without Thunder*. I did several readings for that one and was very close to getting this minor but important role, or so it seemed up until the last minute. I was a Swedish abortion doctor in a frightening future when abortion rights of women in the USA were taken away and abortion outlawed. The women, who had abortions anyway, would be imprisoned in reformatory establishments, where they were drugged and finally succumbed to vegetative states. The script was very disturbing to read. There were some famous names in the film such as Linda Hunt and others I can't remember. Controversial and low-budget as it was, I think, it only played for a few months in the theaters in San Francisco, but it was very good. It consisted of many one-to-one conversations between people, close-ups on camera, and quite a few monologues. As the doctor in Sweden, where the principal actress goes to have an abortion, I explain to her the ways of this procedure, the pros and cons: "We do not encourage it, but if it is necessary, we do not condemn it. . . ."

The casting director thought I was really right for this part, so she even sent me to see a casting coach, in order to practice the lines even more. However, going to those lengths, unfortunately, only had the effect of confusing me and steering me away from my natural talent. So when the reading came before the director of the film I was all worked up, too nervous, and tried much too hard. I know how doctors sound in Sweden, the inflections of their voices, the attitude, and their thoroughness when they speak. Sometimes, you definitely do not need acting lessons.

I had many more auditions over the years for TV commercials and industrials through casting agents in New York. They were Peter Beilin Agency, Cunningham, Escott & Dipene Agency, and Gilla Roos Agency, to name just a few, and Hanns Wollters, of course. The jobs I got I have already written about, some of them. The following are about the auditions for the bookings I did not get or almost did not get and the ones when I really did waste my time.

First of all, when you have an audition it is better not to take it so personally if rejected. Most of the time, in my experience anyway, it is a *type* the casting people are looking for. So if you do not fit their idea of a character, be it principal or extra player in a commercial or film, there is nothing you could do about it anyway, so why waste your emotional resources? "Be yourself," the general advice is. "Don't try to emote," "Act your *type*." "Be believable," "Don't try to be somebody you cannot look like."

Sometimes you are hired right from your picture/résumé only. For example, I got an industrial booking for American Express once. They wanted someone looking like a Frenchwoman sitting in front of her flower store. It was left up to the casting director to present a number of picture/résumés, and then one was chosen, without an audition.

In the seventies there used to be a special very successful Palmolive TV commercial for a dish detergent that hundreds of people in the city auditioned for, including me as well as my friend Sarah. At least three times I was called for this one portraying a customer in a nail salon either German-speaking or with a German accent, as "Tilly," the manicurist, advices her to use this detergent in order to soften her chapped hands and rough nails. Every German actress in town must have been up for this one and Sarah was hardly a European type, but she spoke a little German. We used to make endless fun of Tilly and her nail salon, anticipating that at these auditions we would probably be wasting our time. However, you don't want to be uncooperative with the agent who calls you, and why not give it a shot?

Another one was an AT&T spot. This was for a person with a Swedish accent or a Swedish-speaking person, a very vague description given. Oftentimes it has not been decided what exactly is going to be prescribed and how, especially with languages, it seems to me. In this case, it turned out that several different accents and languages were to be tried out and then just a few selected. So it was Swedish versus *Dutch!* My competition. One or the other. However, neither was used in the final commercial!

At yet another AT&T audition, the casting person was not even present. I waited and waited and then became friendly with an older Indian gentleman in a colorful headdress, who was obviously up for an Indian-speaking part. It was only him and me there. Finally, I got up and left, annoyed and amused at the same time. I told Sarah later, "All I saw was an old man in a turban!"

Some commercial auditions are *really* odd. I was once called to speak into the camera about something I had not the faintest idea what it was about. The words made no sense at all, and in front of me were little pieces of rock placed on a chair!

Others can be outright embarrassing, especially, as I

have said, if you are not right for the part. I was once coupled together with a man much younger than I was. In addition to being miscast, I was not feeling well at all. I was drowsy and tired from the wrong kind of sleep aid I had taken the night before. I could barely say my lines, experiencing some mysterious memory loss as well as vertigo. I felt unsteady suddenly and almost lost my balance. It was a scary moment. The young guy just looked at me. Drugs can really backfire.

Another time I could not *read* the lines. There comes a certain time in your life when your eyes will not cooperate so well anymore. I always had excellent vision, and I was not about to bring *glasses* to an audition! The casting person said, when I strained my eyes, "Aimée, you need glasses?" Forget about it. I could not wait to get that one over with and leave.

Some auditions are purely ad-lib and impromptu. I was asked once to be a German schoolteacher speaking to my students about China! This particular casting person was known for her abrasive personality, and I think she invented the scenario just to see if I could do it.

When you get that callback, as I mentioned, it gets serious. Now you have a real chance at getting a lucrative booking. As is known, the pay for TV commercials is in residuals, which are paid in thirteen-week cycles. There is a special company that organizes and takes care of this business. The checks can be in thousands or hundreds or tens or even singles. Huge checks and tiny ones. So-called Class A national commercials are totally different from local ones.

I don't remember the product, but I was auditioning to be a fashion coordinator from Europe and I did very well on the first call. It was easy, a lark. However, when I got the callback and did the exact same reading the second time, I messed it all up. Why is that? You are nervous now, being considered more seriously. Also, it is another day. You may not feel the same or even look as good. The camera picks up the little unnecessary tics and movements, the wrong nuances. The voice can be too shrill or strained or hurried. I, for one, know instantly if I did well or blew it all to pieces! It's a matter of much discussion and anxiety for actors.

One quite intriguing call I was up for was an American Express commercial. They wanted an Ingmar Bergman feel and look. The casting agent had erroneously told me Ingrid Bergman. The scenes were to be take-offs of Ingmar Bergman's famous films, such as *The Seventh Seal,* in which Max von Sydow plays chess with Death. So here we were, in this little studio, one man and one woman at a time, playing couples in their forties in dreamlike poses, staring out into space, contemplating the agony of life?! I was asked to speak in my native tongue into the camera in order to create some kind of Bergmanesque atmosphere. What it all had to do with American Express I fail to understand.

I got my callback, and at the second audition we were four couples left. This time, I think, I spoke too much Swedish, and the audition had lost its magic, at least for me.

I never saw the commercial on air, but someone told me that he had seen two silhouettes in a dark landscape à la Bergman in a very short Amex spot.

15
Working with Woody

The first time I met Woody Allen was on the set of *Annie Hall*. Buddha had sent me over because they needed a game show demonstrator for a particular scene. "Dress in something very bright, orange or yellow or pink [!]" Buddha told me. What was obviously required was a perky young girl, who was jumping up and down with delight in this game show. Woody Allen was probably making a satire out of it. Well, I was hardly any of the above. It was the most peculiar situation. Woody took one look at me, lowered his head, looking down at the floor, stroked his chin a little, and mumbled something unintelligible. That was apparently often Woody's way. He seemed shy but endearing. And then he just walked away. Someone said, "That was the quickest thirty dollars you ever made, I bet." Oh, yes. At the time, that was the extra SAG player rate for the day.

From my experience the way Woody Allen works: He shoots a lot of scenes and then cancels them or cuts and often changes his mind and then later reshoots them. In the movie *Annie Hall* I don't recall any game show scene at all.

The next time I would be seeing Woody was for a fabulous film, called *The Front,* in which he was acting but not directing. I was an extra player in a party scene, dressed in an absolutely beautiful dress that looked like a tutu. It was mauve organza with silk trimmings, and my hair was made up like a ballerina's. I had a wonderful time on the set and made a lot of friends in the business with whom I later would work many, many times in upcoming films. The casting director at the time was a lively and sanguine Italian man by the name of Ricardo, who had a casting office along with another casting person, who was known as a real lady, Esther Navarro. They had, by the way, also cast me in *Arthur.* Buddha said, "Ricardo is the kind of individual if capsizing in a ship and everyone were about to drown, he would say, 'Let's have a party!' " Most everything was easygoing with him, except for one thing: no arriving late for a booking. I saw him fire someone on the spot once for being a half hour late; "We cannot use you now!" Ricardo was funny. One time he got the idea to send me for an audition as a look-alike for Marilyn Monroe! Esther gasped and protested, "Ricardo, does she look like M.M.?"

The most amazing location I have ever experienced was in Woody Allen's *Stardust Memories.* The filming was taking place on one of those garbage dumps, mountains of them, somewhere outside New York. Was it Staten Island? I never saw such huge mounds of compressed garbage in my life. There were swarms of scavenger birds flying above us, screeching like crazy. We were not there just to be placed next to the garbage. Up the hills we had to climb, and we tripped and tramped and hobbled all the way up, on the stinking ground. This was to be a certain take of a scene in the film about a dream that you were in hell as opposed to heaven. The privileged people go to heaven and the others to hell? I was dressed as a "heaven person" in a shimmering white kind of wrap. Was I lucky? Holding my angelic-looking dress up over the knees and shod in heavy boots for protection, I climbed up and up and just stood there at an angle on the mound for a while during the shooting. But then we had to climb up and down again for the retakes, I don't remember how many times. I think there were train cars somewhere, in which we were riding, we, the privileged. However, I do not remember a single person from "hell!" Woody was there and seemed to be deep in thought and not saying much at all. "Don't talk to him; never talk to him!" we had been told.

Moving on to the eighties. *Scenes from a Mall* it was called, starring Woody Allen and Bette Midler, directed and produced by Paul Mazursky. It was unquestionably one of the best and longest and most income-producing films I have ever worked in. The action in the film takes place in only one day. We were cast by the director himself (and Woody Allen as well), as people shopping in this mall, walking around all over the place, in and out of stores and restaurants and bars and movie theaters, appearing as the same people "throughout the day." Therefore we had to be more or less present during the entire shooting schedule, and the look was important because we would be so often on camera.

The filming took place in a magnificent studio with replicas of all the stores and restaurants, especially built up for the film, somewhere up in Connecticut, and lasted for up to three months. The story actually takes place in California, but that is not Woody's turf, as we know. He wanted to shoot in New York like always, luckily for all the players.

As for me, I was able to fly my regular schedule and work in the movie at the same time because the AD would ask us every day if we could return the following day or not. I ended up working for two months all together. They were very long days and very lucrative, i.e., overtime galore. And then, best of all, we sometimes had martinis at the end of the day in the nearby bar.

Suddenly one day they called my name. I was given a little special action to do, which was to stand in a rising elevator next to Woody and Bette Midler and Fabio, the well-known Italian model, who had a small role. Bette looks up at him in the shot and mentions something about a "younger man," he looks straight ahead, a little bored, like you do in elevators, and I do the same. For some reason I had an excruciating headache at the time, and it really shows on the film in such a way that I appear irate about something. Stressful shopping in a mall?

Bette Midler was very personable and commented on my banana clip in my hair, "I love your hair clip!" Woody was holding on to a huge surfboard, mumbling his words both on and off-camera, as was his way. I really like him; he is so gentle.

I have worked in many more Woody Allen films, the last one being *Small Time Crooks*. It was a very hot day, and we were dressed in elegant party attire. I was given a dove gray chiffon dress by the wardrobe department that swung around my legs when I walked. We were all gathered up in posh town house in the middle of Manhattan. It had these stairs we had to walk up and down a hundred times in the ninety-degree heat. The hum of the air-conditioning had to be halted during shooting, and the hot lamps were torturing us.

But I was together with my old friends in the business. There is something comforting and comfortable in working with the same people over and over again, like family. "Oh, here we are again. . . ." "Did you work on that film?" "I was up for a commercial. . . ." "How was the audition?" "Did you go to that call?" "I worked as a stand-in on *Law and Order* a few days last week." "We made golden time the other day." "How are you doing?" "Terrible!"

16
"Acting" like a "Stewardess"

"Go fly!" Sylvia Fay said when I had to reject one of her calls because my flying schedule conflicted. She meant it lightheartedly, but I hated to say no to a shoot. Was I to feel guilty toward her or to Pan Am? It was sometimes hard to make up my mind. I was always busy trying to move my schedule around. The so-called Open Time Board in Pan Am scheduling, where a lot of swapping and trading of trips took place, I could not have done without.

Sylvia used to call me a lot and ask me to put on my uniform for a film. There were plenty of airport scenes and inside cabin interiors, whether it be mockups in studios or real airplane cabins. Few airlines, though, were willing to lend out an airplane for a film shoot even for a hefty fee. It was too expensive to keep an airplane on the ground. It only makes money when it flies.

In the movies involving airline scenes that I worked in, most of the time I wore my Pan Am uniform, which at the time looked quite sharp. In the film *Hanky Panky* there is a shot of me walking by in the hotel lobby of the Roosevelt Hotel. I was startled to see, years later, how the whole appearance with hat and gloves and high-heeled shoes gave the impression of a style so different from today, which embraces the "casual" look ad nauseam.

The whole demeanor was different, too. I don't care what they call us: stewardesses, stewards, flight attendants, flight hostesses (in other parts of the world), or pursers, coordinators in flight, flight service personnel, or crew members. The thrill of flying is long gone and will never come back, but I think it is up to or actually behooves the new and young crew members of today to negotiate for themselves working conditions that could bring back some respect for a profession that involves so many security and safety and service responsibilities.

The first time I appeared in my uniform was in a film called *Thieves*. I remember nothing about it except that I had to get permission from Pan Am, whose publicity department was very concerned about image, The "Pan Am Image" was drummed into us repeatedly. It was quite a procedure to communicate between the casting people and the Pan Am supervisors about little details for just a one-day walk-on job in a film that at the time only paid sixty dollars.

Other films in which I appeared as a flight attendant were *Chapter Two, Six Weeks,* and *Table for Five.* In the last one, Pan Am as a whole is featured, and the nostalgia really grips you. Maybe you get a little lump in the throat when the famous logo appears. In that one five other "real" flight attendants were actually hired by Pan Am itself for the airport scenes. They were younger than I was and much perkier and fresh-faced, as opposed to me, the older and more "seasoned" one. Anyway, we worked in different scenes. I was seated behind the principal actors at a table, miming a conversation (which is what background players do), while the five others had to open jetway doors and stand around for decoration. There had been a tremendous amount of fuss with the grooming of hairdos and makeup and "regulation-style" uniforms on the part of Pan Am, not the film people. There were supervisors and management personnel all over the set, who were eying us nervously every moment. The Pan Am image was everything.

The shooting was interminably long, with the usual waiting around for the sets to be set up, and when the day finally came to an end one of the flight attendants exclaimed, "Uh, how boring! I hate show business. I would never want to do that again!"

It could actually be quite the contrary. When I was hired for two Italian-made movies shooting in New York for a few days, the airport scenes were very snappy and took only half a day. No overtime there! One was called *Tassinara a New York* (Taxi Driver in New York), an Alberto Sordi film, very funny. It was an airport customs scene, and I was transformed into a passenger this time. The way the Italians shoot! One was on the floor doing something technical in order to avoid being on-camera during the actual shot. They were running around, improvising and gesticulating and having a good time. There were also far fewer workers on the set than in American productions, and they did fewer retakes. More economical no doubt, European style.

The other film was called *Chantilly Express,* cast by who else but Ricardo (Bertoni), the aforementioned Italian casting director, for the New York locations. In this film I was an Italian flight hostess, à la Alitalia, standing at the bottom of the stairs leading into a small plane, greeting passengers. It was like something out of the 1950s I remember as a kid.

I wore so many airline uniforms all through the years in films representing TWA, British Airways, and Air

France, as well as make-believe uniforms, which often were of inferior quality, the fabric very cheap and fitting like they were bought at K Mart. I was a British Airways ground agent in one film, *Coming to America,* and a flight attendant for the same airline in *See You in the Morning.* Those uniforms were very matronly-looking. I was not allowed to appear for a competing airline, but Pan Am did not know. After all, these were hardly starring roles!

Other films I appeared as a flight attendant in were *Quick Change, Sleepless in Seattle, My Father the Hero,* and *Chinese Coffee,* a film with Al Pacino that I never saw. In *Jungle to Jungle* I was a First Class passenger in a mock-up studio witnessing the acting flight attendant exclaiming to Tim Allen, "Excuse me, sir, but your travel companion is peeing on the exit sign!"

In Woody Allen's movie *Everyone Says I Love You* I am an Air France reservations clerk and in *Random Hearts* another transformed ground agent but dressed as a flight attendant, which obviously did not matter very much at all, since the distinctions have become quite blurry as of late. In the scene I put up a somber face listening to the FBI representative making an announcement regarding the search for survivors after an airline crash. I hope that was the last time I ever play an airline person, considering the fact, that I am now too old for that kind of typecasting! At least in my own mind I am, or we will see . . .

17
Pains and Pleasures of the Period Movie

I enjoy some period movies. They are really elaborate affairs, like being made up for a masquerade ball or likewise.

The first one I ever worked in was a made-for-TV movie called *The Dain Curse,* in which I played a temple maiden. I was dressed in some kind of very sheer Egyptian tunic and a headdress. We were all placed in a semicircle around an altar, where Jean Simmons played a priestess of evil worship.

Another TV film I was in was *Little Gloria, Happy at Last* with Bette Davis. I will never forget the magnificent Vanderbilt mansion in upstate New York by the Hudson River, where we were placed on the huge lawn, dressed in 1920s costumes of pastel colors and cloche hats, drinking lemonade.

Yet another one was called *Evergreen,* also for TV, in which we had on 1930s dresses and hats, exquisitely made, the real thing. These wardrobe companies specialize in period clothing. Some pieces look like they came out of museums. I don't know how they manage to maintain the clothing so well, after all the wear and tear it is subjected to on movie sets.

That's Adequate, for TV, was another amazing example of costumes used. I had on a nineteenth-century gown, cape, and hat from Imperial Russia. In the very same film I was also made up as an Egyptian woman à la Cleopatra but blond. My hair was curled with hot tongs and stood out to the sides. I wore it like that for weeks.

One fun job I got was as a 1920s "lady of the night." The film was *Izzy and Moe* with Jackie Gleason and Art Carney. I was wearing a *very* glamorous shimmering and very heavy dress along with long strands of pearls and other period jewelry. The scene was a nightlong party on a boat belonging to a bootlegger. We were his guests, four men and four "playgirls" drinking and dancing and living it up. Suddenly the gangsters arrive, one gunshot, and the party is over.

More period films later, regular screen features:

In *The House on Carroll Street* I played an Eastern European emigrant, a departure from my usual "image." I was made up as a poor and downtrodden woman in a shabby dress and hat and threadworm coat of the forties. We were immigrants en masse entering the United States alighting from a ship in a dock area in New York and queuing up to show our papers, hauling dilapidated suitcases.

One of the most interesting period films I ever worked in was Martin Scorcese's *Age of Innocence.* This was the nineteenth century. Your hair could not be highlighted in the current style, so mine had to be temporarily dyed brown, and this only for a one-day shoot. It was dyed on the same day as the shoot, because the way I had prepared it myself was not good enough for the look. My hair was twisted and pulled as well by the impatient hair people, who had to fit it all under a hat that was difficult to fasten on top of all the pins and swirls. I was annoyed. Finally, an excellent Italian stylist, who was in charge of it all, tilted the hat forward a little, so it looked great.

The costume was something of a wonder, whalebones and all! My midriff was corseted beyond breathing ability almost. There were all these heavy skirts as well as a fitted topcoat extending out at the back, protruding nineteenth-century style. One of the female PAs (production assistants) made us laugh. She shook her head and said, "Lady, you've got a *big ass!*"

We were couples promenading in the Bronx Zoo behind an aviary, where the principal action was taking place.

I have to note that I cannot figure out how the ladies went to the bathroom in that century. No matter how much I tried to lift the costume out of the way, it was jamming me in the sides and around the bust area. I had a very outspoken friend, a wonderful actress, who worked in the film also, and she just blurted out, "I peed all over it!"

On to the nineties, the twentieth century, I mean, if one can keep track of all these ages and eras. This film was originally to be called *Ship of Fools,* and then the title was changed to *The Imposters.* I am not sure which one was more apt. I felt sometimes, while working in it, that I was the fool. However, it was a beautiful and very funny film by the talented Stanley Tucci starring a whole lot of actors. But it was tedious and in the end painful to be in. I had one migraine after another. On the other hand, it was a good booking lasting several weeks, for lots of money, and I certainly did not regret it. Every morning we were made up and had our hair done the same way, 1920s style now. My dress was a silky, slinky long gown, cut on the diagonal, the way they used to, which is very figure-flattering. The makeup was the most important part. The lips and the eyebrows had to be just right. We were upper-class people on a cruise and the studio was set up as a nightclub with an elegant bar, a dance floor, tables and ornate chairs around it as well as a stage with musicians playing and actors singing, who were part of the story line. This location was at the Silvercup Studios in Long Island City. My partner, we were couples, was a very interesting older stage actor who had been around the world just as much as I had. He told stories from China and Korea and of stage work he had done there. After several weeks of being together with the same people twelve hours a day, we had had more than enough of this venture and of each other.

Another ordeal of a booking and far less rewarding was in *The Cradle Will Rock,* a very fine film, by the way. I have never had my hair so mistreated as in that one. It was a hundred years ago again! We had to arrive at the holding area with pincurls on our heads, which they later twisted even further into little swirls that were then flattened as much as possible. On top of that a piece of nylon was forced down and fastened again with more piercing pins. Then on came this ugly wig, period style, and more pins and fasteners. I suffered throughout the night (it was a nightshoot) with this headache, but that was not the worst part. The costume that I had been fitted for, a gray/gold/brown affair, was cutting into my hips in a most uncomfortable way, so I spent the whole time trying to lift it up in order to relieve the pressure. Everyone was fatigued and edgy, being on our feet all night. I was given a great big fan, and my action in the shot was to stand there fanning myself and talking/miming to a gentleman. When it was finally over in the wee hours of the morning, it took another hour to get everyone out of costumes and wigs. This time you get paid for also. The "out-time" is then established by one of the ADs, when everyone is ready to go home and has been released; i.e., all the props and wardrobe items have been returned properly and in an orderly fashion.

18
Films of the Nineties—A Different Look

It seemed to me that the films of the nineties were becoming more fast-paced, more violent, and a little erratic and the editing was overdone. The images would be flashing by, the soundtrack much too loud, so it became indigestible, difficult to enjoy, much less remember. When you looked at earlier movies, more attention was paid to details and they were slower paced and therefore much more absorbable. Were moviemakers starting to think that the public got bored very quickly and had the attention span of four-year-olds? Some of the new films out of Hollywood were downright infantile.

At the same time, nonetheless, there were the excellent ones made by good directors such as: *Traffic, Donnie Brasco, Chocolat, American Beauty, The Piano, The Red Violin, Six Degrees of Separation, Carlito's Way,* and *The Crying Game,* to name a few. One of those Hollywood movies was shooting in New York, for a change, namely *Last Action Hero* with Arnold Schwarzenegger. The entire Times Square area was transformed, and a giant rubber inflated doll of the star was erected in the middle of it. Shooting lasted there for several weeks and was certainly good for the city's economy. It was good for my economy also. Several nights I worked in this spectacle of a film, as a news reporter this time. My action in one scene was to hold a microphone to Schwarzenegger's face when he was running out of a movie theater looking for something or someone, calling and gesticulating. We were the newspeople, pushing and misbehaving. Those nights were very long and very cold.

In another take in the same film we were all playing theatergoers running out of the moviehouse in a hazardous wild panic and stampede, because Death had stepped out of the screen suddenly in Ingmar Bergman's *Seventh Seal* and started to advance toward the audience with his scythe. (Maybe he was mad at being cast in a movie within a movie that was so lowly and unbecoming to his dignity!)

Carlito's Way, staring Al Pacino, was a very good film in which I worked as an office worker, also all night long. It was a violent scene, but the baseball bat they used to bash someone's head with, was light as a feather. You always learn something.

Another very fine film I was in was the half French and half American made film *The Proprietor* with Jeanne Moreau. I was sitting in a restaurant at the Plaza, an "upscale" scene. I mention this one because she has always been one of my favorite actresses, so understated and intriguing.

One location I will never forget was in the film *Commandments.* It was way out on Long Island and all the way out on the beach. The time of the year was November, and it was cold! We were just a few background players portraying locals living out there and running out to the edge of the water in complete amazement and reacting to Jonah, from the Bible, coming out of the sea after having been swallowed by the whale. There were two pieces of "the whale" erected on the beach made of wood and plastic in black and positioned at certain angles for the various camera shots. We were there for a few days, huddling in parkas and boots in a tent supplied with heaters. In the shots we would be plodding back and forth in the sand. It was not easy. All you see in the film is some people on a beach very far away, running out to stare at the ocean.

In *Donnie Brasco* I was a patron in a Japanese restaurant seated together with a Japanese gentleman. Our action was to react in horror to screams and thuds coming from the rest room, where an extremely violent scene was taking place. The Mafia hoods were beating up the owner of the restaurant, because he demanded that they take off their shoes in order to comply with Japanese custom. This was a period movie set in the seventies, and my hair was tied into a ponytail with a strand of hair around as fastener, which would always come undone. Al Pacino was in the scene, standing to the side keeping a low profile while guarding the door to the rest room. In scenes like that, they don't shoot it all at once, the way it looks in the movie. The violent takes were done on other days. This was a very good booking. It usually is when there are just a few players who perform and get a little extra exposure. It may not look like much on the screen, but during the actual filming there were a lot of takes involving different angles and close-ups.

One such job around the same time was, when I was hired as a featured silent bit player in the film *Devil's Advocate,* again with Al Pacino, and Keanu Reeves. I was one of the three ex-wives of the murdered businessman attending his funeral in this church scene along with almost the whole cast in the film. We ex-wives walk slowly in procession in the church aisle to the accompaniment of organ music. The wardrobe department had given me a beautiful designer cape over a black dress and combed my hair in a French twist and applied perfect makeup. I felt pretty good. Then all of a sudden Al Pacino, who was leading the procession, created an extra take, in which he leads me into one of the pews. It was reshot several times. He was very gallant, and I walked into the pew with downcast eyes, in mourning. Afterward, to my mild astonishment, he came over to me, shook my hand, and said, "It was a pleasure!" It does not happen very often, that a major star addresses a minor player like that, but he is a very sympathetic person, joking with people between takes and very personable and obviously fond of women. Unfortunately, my scene with him was cut out.

Other well-known films I worked in during the nineties included *The First Wives Club* (a restaurant scene), *Meet Joe Black* (a street scene, where I walk next to Anthony Hopkins right into the camera), *Analyze This* (a book-signing party, which was cut out), *Mickey Blue Eyes* (never on camera, but several weeks on it), *The Thomas Crown Affair* (another restaurant scene), and many others. In the nineties I started to reject a lot of the calls, partly because I became more selective and partly because I had acquired enough credits to qualify for the minimum pension in the Screen Actors' Guild. Getting up at four in the morning, freezing in the rain or sweltering in the heat, may be impossible to avoid in show business altogether, but I don't have to accept jobs that involve crowd scenes and other uncomfortable or unpleasant conditions.

Grant Wilfley, the casting director, gave me some very good bookings, always something featured. In the film *Pollock,* directed by, starring, and produced by Ed

Harris, I was cast as a background player, featured as the Bejewelled Lady. I was fitted in 1950s clothes, a somewhat dowdy-looking black cocktail dress and a funny hat, but they made a nice big bun out of my hair. I think I looked a bit like my mother did in those days!

Pollock was an excellent film about the artist Jackson Pollock, who painted very avant-garde art (for those who are not familiar with him). In the fifties, this caused a stir and people were shocked and a little turned off at first, before he acquired his fame. He had a very turbulent life, and Ed Harris did an amazing portrayal of the man and his anguish and alcoholic outbursts of rage. What a film! It was quite a moment for me to meet Ed Harris. He said hello, shook my hand, and told me, while his direct blue eyes gazed at me very intently, how to move with my bejewelled and gloved arm and hand when the camera came around. It would be a close-up shot of me holding the art pamphlet. The scene took place in an art gallery, where copies of Pollack's paintings were hung all over the walls. We did that simple take. Then later on in another scene I had to walk into the art gallery and sign the guestbook. The woman sitting by the desk had a principal part, and when she addressed me I had to answer her. The soundboom was above us, but I did not bother to ask for an upgrade. Sometimes it is not appropriate, and besides, in the film there is not a trace of this take. A lot of the art gallery scene is cut out. And that's just the way it is in films.

19
Bernie from the Bronx and Other Characters

Bernie is not a regular guy. Bernie is right out of Damon Runyan. Bernie Friedman is a character actor who has been playing bit parts in New York–made features for almost forty years. He has been a friend to me over the years, a little bit of a confidant, an entertaining off and on companion, whether we are sitting in a café or in a deli or walking in the street to or from the SAG office in New York's Times Square area, or working on a movie set. He has a special persona, a sort of soul. Some people are products of their environment only and do not contribute so much more than what is expected of them. Others are a little more worthwhile to be with, because they create an atmosphere of delight. Bernie was the one who kept me laughing in the ice-cold wind on the set of *Hair* down in the Wall Street area in a long time ago.

When we were taking those long walks in the streets of Manhattan, Bernie used to introduce me to his other Runyonesque actor friends by the names of Bobby Valentine, no longer with us, and Nolan Carley, aka Fishface, maybe because of his small-featured looks. He has done printjobs and TV ads. Peter Condos, aka Peter Perfect, is not a character actor at all but a very good-looking man, who resembles Howard Huges or John Barrymore in the twenties. There is Peter Linari, a heavyset guy who has played many principal character roles from poets to truckdrivers and personified "the big intestine" once! And Peter Leitner, an actor and exceptionally gifted writer, who has done shows on public radio. They all belong to Equity, the stage actors' union, which is located on 46th Street close to SAG in Times Square. I was never a member of Equity, so I do not have access to those premises, unless Bernie is there and can invite me in. There you find all these actors, who are talking about stage work, present and past, off or on Broadway. They have been in the theater all their lives. Some of the women were once very beautiful but now are a little older and, like someone said, "faded stars"! It was actually said in Swedish and loses a lot in the translation.

There used to be a deli restaurant on 46th Street next to Equity, where all the actors congregated and talked about show business. I would sometimes walk in there quickly, looking for Bernie. It was like good therapy, to have a word with him, because he was, shall we say, worlds away from the regulated business of flying on airplanes. He was everything the airline environment was not: witty, carefree, creative, artistic, raucous, seedy, and outrageous. He had a funny name for me: USA, UP-scale Aimée, just like he had invented the other names, Fishface and Peter Perfect. Bernie's conversations are peppered with quips and puns and always of course in a Bronx jargon and accent. Here are three poems of a different kind that he wrote and that one can reflect upon a little.

If I Were a Burger

Wouldn't it be neat, oh golly, what a treat
If I were a burger everyone could eat
I'd come well done or medium rare
When you have
your dinner,
I might well be there
All dressed up in onions, relish and slaw
I'd have to be someone the world would adore
Oh, to be with catsup, the pickles and fries
If I were a burger and not one of the pies

We Esoteric Scalawags

We esoteric scalawags
Who pace the floor with zigs and zags
And light the Moon with such pretense
Can all our lives be so immense?

Such esoteric scalawags
Who carry milk in plastic bags
Then smoke and choke till it's no joke
Yet have time for a few more drags

The children play at Blind Man's Bluff
The cockatoo can't say enough
And still you think you had it rough
Now what about that poor Macduff

The students with their college loans
So many with their handheld phones
The ones who love to wave the flags
Oops, esoteric scalawags

Now we conclude this maze of mist
And sing a tapdance on our wrist
Enjoy the riches and the rags
You biomedic
Tricosmetic
Esoteric scalawags

A Zero, a Zero

A zero, a zero, that's what you are
But my god, sir, I'm a hero
No, my friend, you're a zero
You're no John Glenn or Robert De Niro
But my god, sir, I must insist I'm a hero
A hero never, a liar yes
A pompous ass, I must confess
But sir, why do you degrade me?
What can you possibly gain?
I only speak of what I see
A man who's lost and so inane
So have some wine and soon forget
Of you for whom there's such regret
And as I dance with a golden elf
I must stop talking to myself

Bernie has played so many principal parts, for example: a hospital patient on a gurney in Martin Scorcese's *Bringing Out the Dead,* a cop opposite Frank Sinatra in the 1968 *The Detective,* a bum in *FX,* having his head shaved in a part in *Quick Change,* and as David Letterman's father on TV in the nineties.

Nolan Carley, Fishface, a darling of a man, I have to say, has played a senile old man in a negligee (!) on Conan O'Brien's show, was a body double for Morley Safer, and once impersonated David Letterman in a commercial along with a cow.

Peter Perfect was my "cavalier" a few times in films. We worked together, cast by Sylvia Fay or Grant Wilfley or Joy Todd, who is now no longer in New York, the last job being in the TV series *Now and Again,* in which Peter got a dayplayer part, as well as in *Sex and the City* and *Goodfellas,* the movie. Why is he called Perfect by Bernie? Besides being good-looking, Peter is well dressed, well spoken, very, very kind, and a complete gentleman. He can be flirtatious, making you smile and laugh and blush all at the same time.

Another actor I feel I must mention from many years ago but who has recently resurfaced is Richard Dubois, with whom I worked in the past. We had a prominent walk-on scene in *The Fan,* him trailing behind me in this party scene. I remember especially there was a lot of "playing in the background" around that film job. Richard was living in a Soho loft at the time. I had a Swedish friend, Christina, who came along one evening for a little "partying" in Soho. There were all kinds of call-it-stimulants available at the time, and "under the influence" I never saw such droopy eyes on a person as on my friend, Christina, that evening!

Richard has recently done stand-in work for Robert De Niro in a film and has a lot of former film credits, for example in *Tootsie* opposite Dustin Hoffman.

Now to my female friends in the business. My friend, Natalie Deutz, looks like a ballerina. She did indeed dance for many years at Luigi's here in Manhattan. Some call her Nat the Cat. However, she does not care much for cats! She is somewhat petite, exquisite-looking, with a very well-proportioned figure and a small sculpted face with white hair pulled back in a bun, and is always very elegant. She dresses her part in all her movie calls, "upscale" calls, party scenes and so on. She has had plenty of bit parts in the past, for example in the film *Six Degrees of Separation*. We have worked in so many films together, of which the most memorable one was *Scenes from a Mall*. Since we were working in this film such long days, the end of them would turn into martini parties at the nearby bar. "Let's have a *martini!*" Natalie would exclaim. I would have mine straight up, and hers was on the rocks. Her capacity for drinking was remarkable. She drank me "under the table" once, or at least we stumbled out of the place, somewhere in the city in the middle of the night, after having worked for three days in *First Wives Club*. We sat there, in this elegant bar, two ladies feasting on martinis in huge glasses with olives and thin little pizza slices. We talked and laughed until the world was turning upside down! In the taxi ride home, my head was going in one direction and my legs in another. I spent the rest of the night paying for the pleasure. But Natalie, she was just fine!

The other story with Natalie concerned our pee problems. Every time we were called to the set, Natalie burst out, "I have to pee; isn't that something!" It did not matter how many times we had already visited the ladies' room; we had to go and go again and again, especially before the shooting. That was probably psychological, because once you were placed on the set it could take hours before you would get a break. Contagious as it is, we were both running to the bathroom, her and/or me, and it became a constant preoccupation.

Many of the women I have worked with in films, as well as some of the men, are models and/or ex-models, still very good-looking, and in excellent shape and remarkably well preserved. As Natalie once remarked,

"You can be any age . . . but you *have* to look good!" You have to take care of your skin, your figure, your hair, and unquestionably some imperfections have to be corrected with plastic surgery. Exercise and properly balanced eating habits and enough sleep are essential. You don't exactly eat french fries! You don't even think about it! And you don't talk about it, either! Forget about it! Just eat when you are hungry. The rest of the world is slimmer than Americans, because they serve themselves smaller portions, period. They eat everything, but less of it and not so often, and don't need to be "entertained" so often by TV, either, or other "instruments" of leisure. Actors are always looking for work. That will keep you running and not sedentary!

There is Victoria, a stunning model/actress, who has been in the business for a long time, and Anita, a beautiful German model, who works all the time. And many others I have worked with for so many years, who still look magnificent.

Violetta is quite special, sophisticated, I think an Angelica Huston type. Violetta is one of the most theatrical individuals I have ever met. She is Hungarian and in this accent describes emphatically her experiences, provoking laughter with her many dramatic expostulations. This lady cannot resist a cat in need. A passionate animal lover and animal rights advocate, she has been the caretaker and "mommy" to an impressive number of felines throughout the years. Along with her husband, residing with her have been between ten and twenty cats at any given time, their names lovingly applied: Rosario, Amalia, Manuelita, Orfeo, Simonetta (Violetta often attends the ballet and opera!), Morris, Pancho, Rafael, Leonardo, Mariana, Ildiko, Felipe, Grisito, Pantera, Arubita, Spunky, Fat Fritz, Gwendolin, Simba, Pinguino, Sabrina,

Gabriela, Zoltan, Carboncito, Bello, Amina, Alfonso, Pedro, Margarita, Pabloll (that is number two!), Pamika. So There, Take That, and . . . Bless her soul for being so humane!

Most actors are indeed animal friends. Thank goodness for the influence they can exert, like Doris Day and Brigitte Bardot and so many other stars.

Another friend, Penny Gaston, is a clever, tall, blond, attractive, and quite experienced actress. She has a background onstage as well as in films and TV. She is very outspoken and does not mind correcting a person promptly when she feels that the truth has not been presented properly. She is a whiz at doing crossword puzzles. Women's love lives could be a matter of much discussion, as she once asked me if I ever had been "obsessed" over a man! Well, of course, naturally! The subject of men is perpetually perplexing. They turn you on, and they turn you off! One story she told me was just so unbelievable. How could it be anatomically possible! She is adamant and truthful and swears by it: "Just like a pencil! Just like a pencil!" She is referring to a date she once had. They were necking, as she said, and suddenly "He whipped out this antenna, and it was just like a pencil!" and she demonstrated with her index finger. As I said, she is the most accurate of people.

20
New York 2002–2003—a City Changed? The More It Stays the Same?

For about six months after the tragedy of 9/11 the city had taken on a somewhat dignified and somber and more quiet note. The traffic became more disciplined; people walked a little slower, their facial expressions more reserved. One did not hear the usual loudmouths or the cursing in the streets or the angry expletives in the traffic from one driver to another. The tourists were flocking to the downtown area with varieties of camera equipment gawking at "ground zero" for a little too long. At first it appeared offensive, then it became more acceptable, for ground zero has now become a memorial. That sacred ground is forever changed, whatever will become of it, and so it seems the entire downtown area has also been transformed. When you walk around there . . . I was looking at apartments one day, and the perception was of a town, a different kind of town. Battery Park, Wall Street, the little cobblestone lanes, the parks, and the characteristic architecture of the place, a town *within* a city. Here and there it reminds me of a town in another country, but then around the corner there is New York again.

Now, a year and a half later, the rest of the city is back to "normal"! The traffic is gridlocked, worse than before. Pedestrians are storming forward barely missing hitting one another, when chattering away on their cellphones plastered to their ears like leeches. Shrill voices, restless laughter, and the languages spoken! At Macy's the other day, all I heard was French! I may be nostalgic, but I preferred New York in the seventies. It had more character, a "film noir." It was in black-and-white and suspenseful. Today it is in "Cinemascope with colors," larger, noisier, more populous, and, God forbid, more "suburban"! Middle-class families have settled down here. Pardon me, but I thought this was an *adult* city. How can you push a babystroller through these streets, let alone raise children here? People bring babies into bars! Late at night! Family values gone where? Am I out of date? OK.

And where have all the movies gone? There used to be one production after another, the Upper West Side or midtown streets flooded in glaring camera lights day and night and PAs politely trying to ward off passersby from walking on to sets, "Could you please stay to the left! Thank you, sir! Hold on for a second, while the camera is rolling . . ." or not so politely, "Keep back! Stop right there! Don't walk!"

I finally worked in three movies this year. *Maid in Manhattan, Two Weeks Notice,* and *How to Lose a Guy in Ten Days,* all of them upscale scenes involving gowns and evening makeup and hairdos. I had been partially absent from the business for a year and a half, devoting time to moving in and out of apartments.

Coming back and working in Manhattan-made films

again, I was not so surprised that nothing had changed. Everybody was just a little bit older, including me. I have now had new head shots taken, which is recommended every two to three years in this business, and printed a new "age range" on my résumé, the closer to your real age the better, and reregistered with two casting agencies. The stock markets have "crashed," the economy is weaker, the film shoots are few in New York, and the commercial productions are down somewhat. Let's see how I am doing now!

One of the advantages about show business is that you can stay in it for a very long time, into your fifties, sixties, and seventies. There will always be roles for middle-aged and older people. Also, while you are collecting a SAG pension you can work. However, if you earn over a certain amount of money in film work you do have to notify the guild office, and your pension will be temporarily suspended.

I check my answering service several times a day. See there, I just got a call for a commercial audition!